Baedeker's

SAN FRANCISCO

Imprint

107 colour photographs
6 special plans, 5 graphic illustrations, 3 ground plans
1 transport plan, 1 large city map

Conception and editorial work:
Redaktionsbüro Harenberg, Schwerte
English language: Alec Court

Text and pictures:
Carin Drechsler-Marx

General direction:
Dr Peter Baumgarten, Baedeker, Stuttgart

English translation:
Babel Translations, Norwich. Revision: Wendy Bell

Cartography:
Georg Schiffner, Christoph Gallus, Lahr
Rand McNally & Co., Chicago, IL. (city map)

Source of illustrations:
Drechsler-Marx (96), Historia-Photo (1), Messerschmidt (11)

Following the tradition established by Karl Baedeker in 1844, sights of particular interest and hotels and restaurants of particular quality are distinguished by one or two asterisks.

To make it easier to locate the various sights listed in the "A to Z" section of the Guide, their coordinates on the large map of central San Francisco are shown in red at the head of each entry.

Only a selection of hotels, restaurants and shops can be given: no reflection is implied, therefore, on establishments not included.

In a time of rapid change it is difficult to ensure that all the information given is entirely accurate and up to date, and the possibility of error can never be completely eliminated. Although the publishers can accept no responsibility for inaccuracies and omissions, they are always grateful for corrections and suggestions for improvement.

4th Edition 1992

© Baedeker Stuttgart
Original German edition

© 1991 The Automobile Association
United Kingdom and Ireland

© 1992 Jarrold and Sons Ltd
English language edition worldwide

US and Canadian Edition Prentice Hall Press

Distributed in the United Kingdom by the Publishing Division of The Automobile Association, Fanum House, Basingstoke, Hampshire, RG21 2EA.

The name *Baedeker* is a registered trademark
A CIP catalogue record for this book is available from the British Library.

Licensed user:
Mairs Geographischer Verlag GmbH & Co., Ostfildern-Kemnat bei Stuttgart

Printed in Italy by G. Canale & C. S.p.A. – Borgaro T.se – Turin

0-13-063637-1 US & CANADA
0-7495-0409-9 U.K.

Contents

Alcatraz Island · The Anchorage · Angel Island State Park · Bank of America · Bank of California · Berkeley · Cable Cars · California Historical Society · California Palace of the Legion of Honor · The Cannery · Carmel · Chinatown · Chinese Culture Center · Civic Center · Cow Hollow · Embarcadero Center · Ferry Building · Fisherman's Wharf · Fort Point National Historic Site · Galleria at Crocker Center · George R. Moscone Convention Center · Ghirardelli Square · Golden Gate Bridge · Golden Gate National Recreation Area · Golden Gate Park · Grace Cathedral · Haas-Lilienthal House · Jackson Square · Japantown · Justin Herman Plaza · Lombard Street · Maiden Lane · Market Street · Mexican Museum · Mission Dolores · Monterey · Mount Tamalpais · Muir Woods · Napa and Sonoma Valleys · National Maritime Museum Park · Navy/Marine Corps/Coast Guard Museum · Nob Hill · North Beach · Oakland · Octagon House · Old Mint · Pacific Stock Exchange · Pier 39 · Pioneer Hall · Presidio · St Mary's Cathedral · San Francisco African-American Historical and Cultural Society · San Francisco Fire Department Pioneer Memorial Museum · San Francisco–Oakland Bay Bridge · San Francisco Zoo · Sausalito · Sigmund Stern Grove · Skyscrapers · Spreckels' Mansion · Stanford University Museum of Art · Telegraph Hill · Tiburon · Transamerica Pyramid · Twin Peaks · Union Square · Vedanta Temple · Victorian Houses · Wells Fargo History Museum · World of Oil, Chevron · Yosemite National Park

Airport · Banks · Beaches · Boat tours · Bookshops · Breakdown patrol · Business hours · Churches · Consulates · Crime · Currency · Customs regulations · Drugstores · Electricity · Emergency calls · Events · Food and drink · Galleries · Getting to San Francisco · Hotels · Insurances · Language · Lost and found · Movies · Museums · Music · Newspapers and periodicals · Nightlife · Postal services · Programme of events · Public holidays · Public transportation · Radio, TV · Railroads and buses · Rent-a-car · Restaurants · Shopping · Sightseeing tours · Sports · Taxis · Telephone and telegrams · Theatres · Time · Tipping · Tourist information · Travel documents · Useful Telephone Numbers at a Glance · Weather reports · Weights and measures · Youth hostels

The Principal Sights at a Glance

Preface

This Pocket Guide to San Francisco is one of the new generation of Baedeker city guides.

Baedeker pocket guides, illustrated throughout in colour, are designed to meet the needs of the modern traveller. They are quick and easy to consult, with the principal sights described in alphabetical order and practical details about opening times, how to get there, etc., shown in the margin.

Each guide is divided into three parts. The first part gives a general account of the city, its history, population, culture and so on; in the second part the principal sights are described; and the third part contains a variety of practical information designed to help visitors to find their way about and make the most of their stay.

The new guides are abundantly illustrated and contain numbers of newly drawn plans. In a pocket at the back of the book is a large city map, and each entry in the main part of the guide gives the co-ordinates of the square on the map in which the particular feature can be located. Users of this guide, therefore, will have no difficulty in finding what they want to see.

Facts and Figures

General

San Francisco is the third largest city – after Los Angeles and San Diego – in the state of California, and is the 13th largest city in the United States of America.

On longitude 122°26'27" W and latitude 37°45'10"N, it lies on the Pacific West Coast of the United States.

Situation

Greater San Francisco covers a total surface area of 128 sq. miles (322 sq. km), of which nearly two-thirds is water, and takes in the Californian counties of Tuolumne, San Mateo, Kern, Fresno and Monterey.
The actual city of San Francisco, which includes the outlying counties of Marin in the N, San Mateo in the S and Alameda and Contra Costa in the E, has a population of about 741,000

Area and Population

The city has a central administration which is headed by a Mayor who comes up for election every four years.
The Mayor is aided by a chief executive administrator, the counterpart, albeit with lesser powers, of the City Managers found in many other American cities. The Board of Supervisors, the equivalent of a single chamber for local government, consists of 11 elected members.
The city's current constitution dates from 1931 but has been subject to over 400 amendments which makes it some 110,000 words long.

Administration

Population

The population of San Francisco originally grew very slowly and in 1846, which saw the end of Mexican rule, amounted to barely a thousand. This dropped to a few hundred in the years that followed – in 1847 San Francisco had a population of 459 which included 22 English, 27 Germans, 14 Irish, 14 Scots, 228 native-born Americans and 89 "Californians".

Population

The Gold Rush in 1849 sparked off a population explosion for San Francisco. Only a year later the population figures had climbed to an estimated 25,000 and by 1890 they stood at almost 300,000. After reaching 342,000 in 1900 they fell away, after the Earthquake in 1906, to 175,000. By 1910 San Francisco's population had climbed again to 416,000, in 1920 it was 506,000 and in 1950 it peaked at 775,000. The last 35 years have seen San Francisco's population decline by about 100,000, owing primarily to people moving out of town to live in the surrounding countryside. The 1980 census declared a total population of 679,000, the lowest since 1950, but since then there has been an increase. The current

◄ *Golden Gate Bridge, synonymous with San Francisco*

People of San Francisco

official estimate puts the number of inhabitants at 741,000. The number of whites plummeted disproportionately from almost 700,000 in 1950 to less than 450,000. The rest of the city's population includes over 100,000 blacks, 85,000 Chinese, 30,000 Filipinos, 14,000 Japanese, 3500 Indians, as well as Koreans, Vietnamese, Samoans, Malaysians, etc. It comes as no surprise to learn that San Francisco has a larger Asian population than any other American city.

Ethnic variety

Apart from the many Asians in their number, the people of San Francisco hail from a host of different ethnic back grounds. When figures on the national origins of San Franciscans were compiled over ten years ago it emerged that 42% of the city's children did not speak English in their homes: 9% spoke Spanish at home, 4·2% Italian, 3·7% German and 1·8% French. The number of Spanish-speaking families is likely to have increased considerably since that time.

San Francisco even has a small Russian enclave around Clement and Geary Streets, while most blacks live in the area of Western Addition. Another indication of the unusually broad ethnic variety of San Francisco is the number of restaurants offering foreign cuisine.

Gays form one of San Francisco's most prominent, as well as militant, minorities. They are well organised and also politically very active. When in 1978 the Mayor of the time and the city's first homosexual Supervisor were gunned down by a disgruntled ex-colleague who then got off with a relatively light sentence, the city erupted in days of civil clashes, and the situation only quietened down when the new Mayor, Dianne Feinstein, nominated another gay to take the murdered Supervisor's place. A survey published at the end of 1984 showed 40% of San Francisco's single men to be homosexual. The rapid spread of AIDS – by 1987 about 70% of the city's gay community were found to be HIV positive – has had a profound effect on the homosexual scene. Fear of infection has come increasingly to influence the social climate while on the political front there are ever greater demands for further action to combat the disease and to fight discrimination against AIDS sufferers and those infected with the AIDS virus.

Gays

San Francisco was also in the forefront of change when it became the first home base for the beatniks and hippies who then expanded their movement to many other cities. It was also the breeding ground for more unsavoury phenomena such as the Symbionese Liberation Army and the sect led by the fanatical Jim Jones – violence has never been a stranger to this, the first city to spring from the Wild West.

Cults and movements

Like almost every city in the USA San Francisco also boasts a host of different religions. It is the seat of a Catholic Archbishop and of the Episcopalian Bishop for the whole of Northern California. San Francisco has two Russian Orthodox cathedrals and places of worship for almost every religious denomination found in the United States. The largest Lutheran congregation is that of St Mark's near St Mary's Cathedral. The city has long been a hotbed for religious sects, of which the most notorious was the People's Temple. Its leader, Jim Jones, succeeded in attracting a large number of idealistic followers, drawn mostly from the blacks and the poor, and led them on to mass suicide in Guyana. In the early 1970s Zen Buddhism gained its first foothold in the States in San Francisco, mainly through the books of Alan Watts, a former Anglican priest who ranks as the foremost exponent of Oriental religions in the Western World.

Religion

Transport

San Francisco Bay provides the city with a natural harbour which, although at one time America's principal port for trade

Port

with the Far East, in recent years has lost much of its earlier importance. Nowadays many of the 46 piers (on both sides of the Ferry Building) stand empty or out of commission. The tonnage has dropped to 2·5 million tons a year and the number of vessels discharging their cargo here is only 850 a year. Back in 1969 the port of San Francisco had already been overtaken by Oakland on the other side of the bay, which has since increased its lead, made up predominantly of container traffic. The San Francisco fishing industry has also declined considerably.

Airport

The airport 14 miles (23 km) S of the city was opened in 1927 as Mills Field which, with expansion, changed its name to San Francisco Airport and finally to San Francisco International Airport. Today it is one of the largest in the United States and serves over 34 airlines. There is another airport at Oakland on the east side of San Francisco Bay.

Railways

Like many American cities, rail transport has, for San Francisco, become almost insignificant, with only one station which handles commuter traffic and the CalTrain with services to San José. The Amtrak trains that run along the Pacific Coast leave from Oakland and passengers get there by shuttle bus from the Transbay Terminal.

Bus services

San Francisco is served by a large number of local and long-distance bus lines and has two main bus stations – the Greyhound Terminal and the Transbay Terminal.
The bus network serving virtually every part of town is San Francisco's most important form of public transportation. There are 57 routes altogether and the basic fare includes transfers between the different forms of transportation in the MUNI system which also covers the streetcars (trams).

BART subway

San Francisco does not have an underground system as such but in 1981 the four streetcar lines that ran along Market Street were moved underground. They form part of the BART (Bay Area Rapid Transit) subway and surface rail system, whose first line was opened in 1972, linking the heart of San Francisco with the surrounding counties (San Mateo, Contra Costa and Alameda).
There are 31 stations on the 71 mile (114 km) system, eight of them in San Francisco itself. The 3 mile (6 km) stretch that runs under the waters of the bay between San Francisco and Oakland is the longest of its kind in the world.

Streetcars, Cable Cars

Except for New Orleans and Sacramento, the capital of California, San Francisco is the last city in the USA to have retained its trams, or streetcars as they are called in the States. It has five streetcar lines, part of them underground, as well as three cable car lines, a service that dates back over 100 years.

Ferries

The ferries that were needed to cross the bay before the bridges were built have by now almost all gone out of business, but passenger ferries still operate to the bay communities of Larkspur and Sausalito (from the Ferry Building) and to Tiburon, Angel Island and Alcatraz (from Fisherman's Wharf).

You are now entering San Francisco

The cable car – one of San Francisco's top attractions

For passengers only – the ferry across the bay

Highways

Except to the S where Highway 101 provides the fastest direct route to Southern California (the other main roads S are Instate 280 and State Highway 1 which follows the coast), San Francisco relies upon bridges to link it with the rest of California.

Going northwards, Highway 101 crosses the Golden Gate Bridge to Northern California, the NW United States and Canada, with Coastal Highway 1 branching off. Interstate Highway 80 runs E over the San Francisco–Oakland Bay Bridge and Highway 92 passes over the San Mateo Bridge to State Highway 17 and Interstate 680 to the S; State Highway 24 and Interstate Highway 680 also lead N and Interstate 580 proceeds E.

Culture

General

Until about 1960 San Francisco was the undisputed cultural centre of California but it has since had to share this distinction with Los Angeles, which is five times its size.

Today San Francisco has four large theatres and a number of "little" theatres. It has its own opera and, in the San Francisco Ballet, America's oldest ballet company. Its Symphony Orchestra, founded in 1911, moved into the newly built Louise M. Davies Symphony Hall in the fall of 1980.

The city also has several first-class art museums – the M. H. de Young Memorial Museum, the Asian Art Museum, the San Francisco Museum of Modern Art, and the Palace of the Legion of Honor, as well as the important Science Museum

The Main Public Library in the Civic Center

of the California Academy of Sciences, plus many special museums, cultural centres and similar institutions.
At the end of April and in early May – every year an International Film Festival is held, concentrating on the AMC Kabuki 8 Theaters. Started in 1957, it was the first of its kind to be held in America.

The universities most commonly identified with San Francisco are not in the city itself but, in the case of the University of California, in Berkeley and in the case of Stanford University in Palo Alto. Located in the city itself is the University of San Francisco, the oldest academic establishment in the area, which was founded in 1855 as St Ignatius College and is still run by the Jesuits.
The University of California Medical Center in San Francisco is also of considerable importance. Founded in 1964 as a private institution it incorporates the highly respected University Hospital. Other important colleges are the San Francisco State University, the Hastings College of Law, the Lincoln University and the San Francisco Art Institute.

Universities and Colleges

Economy

Unlike Los Angeles, with its oil industry and high industrialisation, and other parts of Southern California, San Francisco has never been in the forefront of industrial cities.
It owes its importance much more to services and tourism.

Banking and Insurance

15

Bird's-eye view of the University of San Francisco with St Ignatius Church

Foremost among its service industries are its banks, which include America's biggest bank, the Bank of America, as well as the Bank of California, the Wells Fargo Bank and the Crocker Bank.

It is also important for its insurance companies, to which it owes its new landmark, the Transamerica Pyramid. In the Pacific Stock Exchange San Francisco also has the most important trading exchange in the American West.

Tourism

Its many hotels and restaurants are of incalculable value to the city's economy. The city is such a magnet that every year it attracts five times as many visitors as the resident population, with almost a third of these three million visitors coming to San Francisco for conventions.

Industry

Industry centred on the port, once the most important sector of San Francisco's economy, has been declining for many years and will probably never recover its earlier importance – the same is true of the city's fisheries and canneries.

Many industrial corporations have their headquarters in San Francisco but their plants in other parts of California, chief among these is Crown Zellerbach.

Depending on the state of the American economy, building and construction also has an important part to play, however, given the rather sporadic activity in this sector in the recent past, massive fluctuations are unavoidable.

The business quarter – heart of commercial San Francisco ▶

Famous People

David Belasco
(25.7.1859–14.5.1931)

David Belasco, one of the most important pioneers of the early American theatre, was born in the cellar of a house in Howard Street. Several years later his family moved to Canada; at the age of six he started his life in the theatre as a child actor with travelling roadshows. In 1880 he tried for the first time, unsuccessfully, to gain a foothold in New York but was subsequently to achieve wide fame as a playwright, director and producer, and the theatre bearing his name still stands in New York today. Belasco was famous as a producer of stage effects and scenery, and also as a discoverer and developer of new talent – many of his discoveries went on to scale the heights of the acting profession. Puccini modelled two of his operas – "Madame Butterfly" and "The Girl of the Golden West" – on stage plays by Belasco.

Isadora Duncan
(27.5.1878–13.9.1927)

Born in the house bearing a plaque to this effect on the corner of Geary and Taylor Streets, the famous dancer Isadora Duncan was raised by her divorced mother. Interested in the dance from an early age, she had only had a few ballet lessons before she developed her own theories and techniques which ran counter to those of classical ballet. Clad in flowing robes, she sought to re-create the dance forms of ancient Greece.

Her first appearance in the States was in Chicago in 1899; although this proved a failure, in Europe she won enthusiastic acclaim. In 1904 she opened a school in Berlin with her elder sister, Elizabeth, and then went on to make her permanent base in Paris. 1905 saw the first of her tours in Russia where, although her disdain for the rules of the classical dance met with little favour, her predilection for improvisation proved more acceptable. The Russians were particularly impressed by her preference for short dance pieces to the music of Gluck and Chopin which no one had previously considered appropriate for interpretation by dance. In 1921 she opened a school in Moscow. Her American tours, of which the last was in 1922, were less successful. Her love affairs were eagerly seized upon by the Press and the American public disapproved of her avowed sympathy for the emergent Soviet State.

Lawrence Ferlinghetti
(b. 24.3.1919)

Born in Yonkers, close to New York City, the poet Lawrence Ferlinghetti studied in Paris at the Sorbonne and came to San Francisco in the early fifties where as author, bookseller and publisher, he had a profound influence on every aspect of the literary life of the city. A poet of the Beat Generation, through his publishing centre, the City Lights Bookshop, he offered the Beat poets the opportunity to become better known outside the confines of California, for example by publishing Allan Ginsberg's first work, "Howl", in 1956.

His own poetry employs unusual speech rhythms, stressed by a highly individual form of typography ("Pictures from The Gone World", 1955; "Her", 1960; "Starting from San Francisco", 1961; "Routines", 1964; "An eye on the world", 1967; "Open eye", 1973, et al.).

This major American poet is more usually associated with New England than the West Coast but Robert Frost was in fact born in San Francisco, where his father worked as a journalist. After her husband's death in 1885 his New England mother took young Robert back E and apart from three years in England (1912–15) Frost lived the rest of his life in the states of Massachusetts and Vermont.

Robert Lee Frost
(26.3.1874–29.1.1963)

He was 40 before he published his first volume of poetry which, with its formal simplicity of language and sensitivity for the everyday life of New England folk, was an immediate success. Ten more volumes followed, as well as several rather unsuccessful plays.

In 1978 San Francisco honoured the poet by dedicating the Robert Frost Plaza, where California Street meets Market Street, and putting up a large bronze tablet with the following four lines of Frost's verse:

> "Such was the life in the Golden Gate:
> Gold dusted all we drank and ate.
> And I was one of the children told
> We all must eat our peck of gold."

The short-story writer Bret Harte, like many other early Californians, hailed from the East Coast. Born in Albany, the capital of New York State, he came to San Francisco in 1853 as a 17 year old shortly after the start of the Gold Rush. He worked for a number of different journals until in 1868 he became editor of the new "Overland Monthly", which within three years he had made one of America's most important literary journals.

Bret Harte
(25.8.1836–5.5.1902)

Its second issue contained his most celebrated work "The Luck of Roaring Camp" in which, as in his other short stories of the time, he sketched episodes from California's pioneering days with an almost brutal naturalism, leavened by an occasional touch of dry humour.

The journal "Atlantic Monthly" put him under contract for the astounding sum, for that time, of 10,000 dollars a year, but his published work in the following eight years (up to 1878) did not come up to his earlier writings. In 1878 he was appointed US Consul in Krefeld, Germany, and subsequently transferred to the Consul's post in Glasgow, Scotland. In 1885 he moved to London where he spent the last years of his life.

Jack (John Griffith) London was born in San Francisco, the illegitimate son of a travelling astrologer, and was raised by an unloving mother and a devoted stepfather. In his mid teens he worked in a cannery and a jute factory before going to sea, returning from which he was for a time unemployed. When in 1896 gold was first struck in the valley of the Klondike River in Canada he joined the hordes who streamed to the area in search of a fortune.

Jack London
(12.1.1876–22.11.1916)

A professed "unscientific socialist", he published his first story in 1898 and went on to write over 40 novels, including what is probably his best-known work "Call of the Wild", and a host of short stories before his suicide at Glen Ellen (California) on 22 November 1916.

Born in San Francisco the son of a Scottish immigrant, Robert Strange McNamara, after graduating from high

Robert S. McNamara
(b. 9.6.1916)

19

San Francisco as it appeared in an engraving of 1852

school in his home town, spent time at a number of colleges and universities, including the University of California in nearby Berkeley. After a relatively short term as assistant professor of economics (1940–3) he entered industry, joined the Ford Motor Company in 1948 and in 1960 became President of this American automobile manufacturer. A year later President Kennedy took him into his Cabinet as his Defense Secretary. Using his experience of business, McNamara tried to make the US armed forces a more effective fighting machine but his measures of reform were impeded by the growing intensity of the war in Vietnam which he began by supporting but ended up opposing. He remained Defense Secretary until 1968 and was President of the World Bank from 1968 to 1981.

Leland A. Stanford
(9.3.1824–21.6.1893)

Born a poor farm boy in a small town in New York State, Leland Amanas Stanford became one of the richest and most powerful men in San Francisco where he lived from his arrival there at the time of the Gold Rush until his death. Stanford sold the gold-seekers food and clothing and often took gold in payment. From these early beginnings he worked his way up to become President of the Central Pacific Railroad and later became State Governor and Senator for California. He built a magnificent mansion on Nob Hill where the Stanford Court Hotel now stands. In memory of his only son who died at the age of 16, he founded what is now Stanford University (begun in 1887 as Stanford College) in Palo Alto, as well as the Stanford University Museum of Art, which originally bore his son's name.

Lincoln Steffens
(6.4.1866–9.8.1936)

The crusading journalist Lincoln Steffens was born in San Francisco and raised in Sacramento, the capital of California, where his family lived in an enormous Victorian house (later to become the Governor's Mansion). After being turned down by Berkeley, he pursued his studies in ` Europe. He made a name for himself while working on several of America's best-known newspapers, as the enemy of corruption in American city politics. After publishing his chief work "The Shame of the Cities" in 1904 he travelled all over the States collecting further material. This brought him back to the city of his birth which, because of its corrupt city government, in which "pro-labour" officials proved to be in the pocket of the capitalist bosses, he singled out for his most savage attacks. In 1927 he retired to Carmel and four years later published his autobiography, setting out his aims for social reform.

Levi Strauss, the German immigrant responsible for the world-famous Levis, the jeans that have been made in San Francisco since 1850, came to America at the age of 14. Before embarking on the three-month voyage round Cape Horn he had stocked up from the store run by two of his brothers in New York with various types of cloth and several bales of sailcloth for use on covered wagons. By the time he got to San Francisco he had got rid of all his goods apart from the sailcloth. On hearing a prospector complaining one day that the hard work was getting his pants ripped, Strauss hit on the idea of having pants (i.e. trousers) made up out of the sailcloth. These sold like hot cakes and in 1853 Strauss and his brothers founded the firm that still bears his name.

Levi Strauss (1829–1902)

The idea of strengthening the pockets of the jeans with copper studs came from a local tailor who patented it jointly with Strauss in 1873. Instead of sailcloth Strauss later used serge from Nîmes, in France, because it was more hard-wearing, and this "serge de Nîmes" came to be called "denim".

History of San Francisco

Juan Rodriguez Cabrillo sails into the waters of what is now known as San Diego Bay and six weeks later sights in San Francisco Bay the Farallon Islands which have formed part of the city since 1872.

1542

Sir Francis Drake is the first European to land on the coast of Northern California, probably on the opposite side of the bay from San Francisco in what is now Marin County. He names the land "Nova Albion" and claims it in the name of Queen Elizabeth I.

1579

Sebastian Rodriguez Cermenho lands in a bay on the Marin coast which he calls La Bahia de San Francisco (now Drake's Bay). This is the first use of the name which was given to the city.

1595

The present San Francisco Bay is discovered by Gaspar de Portola and his troops approaching from the land side. Portola, later to be the first Governor of Spanish California, is leading a "Holy Expedition" northwards from Sonora in Mexico in conjunction with Father Junípero Serra, founder of the mission.

1769

1776   A group of 250 Spanish soldiers and civilians, led by Juan Bautista de Anza, decide on the site for the San Francisco Presidio.
Consecration of the first "Mission Dolores", originally San Francisco de Assisi.

1816   Otto von Kotzebue, the German captain of the Russian ship "Rurik" on a voyage of discovery (with Adalbert von Chamisso also on board as botanist), writes of the degrading treatment of the Indians who had lived in the area since the 2nd millennium B.C.

1835   The Mexicans, who had cast off Spanish rule in 1821, turn down President Andrew Jackson's offer of 500,000 dollars for the bay of San Francisco. In the same year William Richardson, an English whaling captain (married to a Mexican and a convert to Catholicism) founds the village of Pueblo Yerba Buena.

1845   Yerba Buena now numbers some 350 souls – Americans, Indians, Dutch and Spanish.

1846   On 9 July Yerba Buena becomes part of the United States when 70 marines from the US frigate "Portsmouth" land there and hoist the Stars and Stripes in the village square. Three weeks later a ship arrives bringing 238 Mormons in search of their promised Zion; they find themselves back in a different part of the United States, the country where they were trying to leave.

1847   Yerba Buena's first American "Alcalde" or Mayor, Lieutenant Washington A. Bartlett, announces on 30 January that henceforth the town is to be called San Francisco which at this time has a resident population, excluding military and naval personnel, of 459.

1848   While building a windmill for John Augustus Sutter, James Marshall discovers gold on 24 January at Coloma in the foothills of the Sierra Nevada. His discovery sets the seal on the future of San Francisco. When news reaches the outside world, prospectors set out in their thousands for San Francisco which serves as the jumping-off point for the gold fields on the Sacramento River.

1850   San Francisco's population has grown in the interim to 25,000, and it becomes a city. A few months later California becomes the 31st State of the Union.

1851   San Francisco, which two years earlier had been just a speck on the map, ranks fourth in the United States in shipping terms (behind Boston, New York and New Orleans).
Much of the city is destroyed by fire but is soon rebuilt.

1852   Prospectors establish a record as gold to the value of 80 million dollars is recorded.

1854   The city has no less than 20 theatres and 573 saloons – one for every 60 people.
Lola Montez, former mistress of Ludwig I of Bavaria, takes the town by storm.

1859   The city adopts its present seal.

Within a decade the city's population has grown to 56,000 – a process that took New York 190 years, Boston as much as 200 and Philadelphia 120.
The clipper "Andrew Jackson" breaks all records by making the voyage round the Horn from New York to San Francisco in only 89 days.

1860

Opening of the telegraph line direct to New York.

1862

Following smaller earth tremors, San Francisco suffers its first major earthquake on 9 October, followed by a second quake on 23 October which considerably damages the city.

1865

The Central Pacific Railroad completes the building of the railroad from the East Coast to San Francisco, an event that is enthusiastically celebrated in the city.

1869

The City Government decides to build the Golden Gate Park.

1870

On 2 August Andrew Hallidie's brainchild the cable car makes its first trip over the 100-yard stretch of Clay Street between Kearny and Jones Streets.

1873

Opening of the Pacific Stock Exchange.

1875

The Southern Pacific Railroad completes construction of the line from San Francisco to Los Angeles.
500 unemployed demonstrate in front of City Hall, calling on the Mayor to provide work for them.

1876

July sees the first serious rioting against the Chinese. A Citizens' Safety Committee restores law and order.

1877

The American Speaking Telephone Company publishes its first telephone directory for San Francisco.

1878

10,000 trade unionists, including a large number from the Seamen's Union founded in 1880, take part in the biggest labour parade yet seen in San Francisco.

1886

John McLaren, an immigrant Scot, becomes Administrator of the Golden Gate Park, embarking on a 56-year tenure of office which ends only with his death at the age of 94. His influence is decisive in shaping the park.

1887

This day has gone down in history because it was the only day on which snow covered the whole of San Francisco.

5.2.1887

The Golden Gate Park is the venue for San Francisco's first large-scale exhibition, the California Midwinter International Exposition.

1894

Opening of the Ferry Building.

1898

A new city constitution enters into force empowering the City Government to operate the city's water, electricity and gas supply as a municipal undertaking.
The city now has a population of 342,000.

1900

15 new banks are opened within a month; the following year sees the founding of the Bank of America (originally called "Bank of Italy"), now the USA's biggest bank.

1903

Honoured by the city: Juan de Anza (statue), Luisa Tetrazzini (fountain)

President Theodore Roosevelt sends the first message over the new Pacific Cable from San Francisco to the Philippines. The first drive by an automobile from San Francisco to New York; the trip takes 63 days.

18.4.1906

At 5.12 a.m. San Francisco is hit by an earthquake which initially causes less damage in the city than in the towns in the immediate vicinity but the fires started by the quake, fanned by the high winds, reduce three-quarters of the city's homes, hotels and businesses to ashes. 250,000 people are made homeless and find temporary shelter in tents in the Presidio and the city parks. But rebuilding proceeds apace, funded by over 100 million dollars from all over the States.

1907

A plague epidemic is successfully brought under control after several months; the last of the plague-ridden rats is caught in October 1908.

24.12.1910

Christmas Eve sees the celebration of the completion of the rebuilding of the city when Luisa Tetrazzini, San Francisco's most popular performer, sings before an estimated crowd of 250,000 in front of the Lotta Fountain on Market Street.

1911

Founding of the San Francisco Symphony Orchestra.

1915

The great Panama-Pacific International Exposition is opened in Lincoln Park a few months after the first ship to take the new route through the Panama Canal docks in San Francisco.

Alexander Graham Bell makes the first transcontinental telephone call from New York to San Francisco.
Dedication of the present City Hall.

In the course of a longshoremen's strike a bomb explodes during a citizens' Preparedness Day parade on the corner of Market and Steuart Streets, killing 10 people and injuring 40. Two labour leaders, Mooney and Billings, are arrested, convicted and jailed. After more than two decades of agitation, based on the belief that they had been framed, these two were finally to be pardoned and released after spending 22 years in jail. — 1916

The main building of the San Francisco Public Library in the Civic Center comes into use. — 1917

The first party convention to select a presidential candidate takes place in San Francisco. The Democrats nominate James M. Cox and Franklin D. Roosevelt for the Presidency and Vice-Presidency but they fail to win election in November. — 1920

Opening of The M. H. de Young Memorial Museum in Golden Gate Park. Pictures of the Dempsey-Carpentier fight are flown from the East Coast to San Francisco in 48 hours 45 minutes. — 1921

President Warren Harding dies from a stroke in the Palace Hotel four days after arriving in San Francisco. — 1923

The first of the regular mail flights providing a mail service between New York and San Francisco. — 1924

Opening of Mills Field as San Francisco's municipal airport. — 1927

"Graf Zeppelin", the German airship, flies over San Francisco on its way from Tokyo and lands in Los Angeles. — 25.8.1929

Ratification of the City Constitution that is still in operation today. Puccini's "Tosca" becomes the first opera to be performed in the War Memorial Opera House (Civic Center). — 1932

Dedication of the Coit Tower on Telegraph Hill.
The island of Alcatraz becomes a Federal Penitentiary. — 1933

Beginning of the longshoremen's strike that lasts for over two months and ends up by involving all workers in a general work stoppage on 25 May which completely paralyses the city. — 9.5.1934

Opening of the Golden Gate Bridge. Three months earlier ten workers had been killed when a girder collapsed. — 12.11.1936

Opening of the Golden Gate Exposition on Treasure Island. — 1939

One day after Japan declares war on the USA San Francisco experiences its first blackout. — 8.12.1941

Beginning of the evacuation of Japanese residents of San Francisco for internment in camps farther along the coast. — 6.8.1942

Opening of the Founding Assembly of the UNO in the War Memorial Opera House, followed by the signing there two months later of the original Charter. — 25.4.1945

History of San Francisco

1946
During three days of rioting in the penitentiary on Alcatraz two prisoners and three warders lose their lives.

8.9.1951
Yoshida, the Japanese Prime Minister, signs the Treaty marking the ending of hostilities between Japan and the USA in the War Memorial Opera House.

1954
San Francisco International Airport opens for traffic.

1957
The Governor of California signs a Bill setting up the present Bay Area Rapid Transit District consisting of San Francisco and four surrounding counties.

1960
Opening of the San Francisco Asian Art Museum in the Golden Gate Park.
A population census reveals that in the previous ten years San Francisco lost 35,000 residents to the suburbs and now only has a population of 741,000.

22.3.1963
The penitentiary on Alcatraz is closed down. A year later the island is occupied by Sioux Indians who lay claim to Alcatraz.

15.4.1967
One of the first big peace marches against the Vietnam War takes place in Market Street. Others follow at regular intervals.

1971
Two Standard Oil tankers collide in fog under the Golden Gate Bridge, spewing out vast quantities of oil into the Bay. The Indians are driven off Alcatraz.

1974
BART (Bay Area Rapid Transit) takes over transportation between San Francisco and Oakland.

31.3.–8.5.1976
Strike by City Hall employees. Public transportation also comes to a halt during this period.

1977
The San Francisco Bay area is shaken by eight earth tremors, the worst for 11 years.

1978
Opening of Pier 39.
Mayor George Moscone and Harvey Milk, one of the 11 Supervisors, are gunned down in City Hall by an ex-colleague who had been fired by Milk. A week later Dianne Feinstein, Chairperson of the Board of Supervisors, is named as Moscone's successor. She is the city's first woman Mayor.
A Rembrandt and other valuable paintings are stolen from the de Young Museum.

1979
George White, who had shot Moscone and Milk, is sentenced to seven years in jail. The light sentence leads to angry protests resulting in considerable damage to property.
In September the cable cars are taken out of service for several weeks to undergo essential repairs. At the same time BART and the Golden Gate Ferries to Larkspur and Sausalito become strikebound.

The ten-yearly population census reveals that San Francisco's population has continued to decline in the seventies, and, in the 30 years between 1950 and 1980 has fallen from 775,000 to 678,000, i.e. by over 12%.

1980

The three existing cable car lines are temporarily shut down (for two years) to allow a complete overhaul of the system.

1982

Moscone Convention Center south of Market Street between Howard and Folsom, 3rd and 4th Streets, is opened.

Dianne Feinstein is re-elected Mayor with an overwhelming majority.
By a vote of 50·6% to 49·4% the control plan to limit the growth of Downtown San Francisco is defeated.

1983

After 2 years' closure the cable cars come back into service on 21 June; repairs have cost 60 million dollars.
The Democratic Party holds its convention in the new Moscone Center; Walter Mondale is nominated as presidential candidate and Geraldine Ferraro becomes the first woman to stand for the office of Vice-President. In November they lose the election.

1984

For the sixth time an attempt to get a law passed restricting the building of high-rise office blocks is defeated by the electorate with a 52% majority.

1985

The Nobel Peace Prizewinner, Mother Theresa, builds a convent in San Francisco.
At the seventh attempt the electorate votes for the restriction on building in downtown San Francisco. In future not more than 475,000 square feet of building can be started annually.

1986

Several new hotels have changed the appearance of the district around Union Square. Some 16% of available office space is empty; rents are falling for the first time.
The 50th anniversary of the opening of the Golden Gate Bridge is celebrated with great festivity.

1987

After ten years as Mayor Dianne Feinstein is replaced in office by Art Agnos.
Artefacts uncovered in the course of digging the foundations for a new bank on the corner of Kearny and Sacramento Streets point to Chinese settlement in San Francisco prior to 1850.

1988

The Pentagon decides to close the Presidio as an economy measure. San Franciscans are incensed and protest furiously.
On October 17th at 5.04 p.m. (during the rush-hour) the city is struck by the worst earthquake (6·9 points on the Richter Scale) since the earthquake of 1906. The Marina quarter is most badly affected; many houses catch fire as the result of gas leaking from burst mains. A 1¼ mile/2 km section of the San Francisco-Oakland Bay Bridge collapses burying numerous cars.

1989

In June, serious fires, some started deliberately, cause widespread devastation in southern California.

1990

Quotations

Eugene Burdick
American writer
(1918–65)
Three Californias

"The City (San Francisco) is the central part of California. Everything belongs to it from the Techahapis in the South up to the line of Marin County. Above lies the North. The City, San Francisco, is a living miracle, a discovery, something made up and not quite true. Everyone within the orbit of the City 'lives' there. People from Palo Alto, San José, Santa Cruz, Berkeley, Orinda, Piedmont, Atherton and Oakland always say to outsiders that they're from the City – I mean, from San Francisco" . . .
There are three Californias – Northern, Southern and The City. Each one is made up of people come in from other States. But they don't simply come to California, they come to one of these three Californias."

Duke Ellington
American Jazzman
(4.7.1899–24.5.1974)

"San Francisco is one of the great places for culture in the world . . . a really urbane community in the USA, a really cosmopolitan place, and over the years it's always been set to welcome anyone from anywhere."

Lawrence Ferlinghetti
American poet
(b. 24.3.1919)

"San Francisco looked like an island, with the white houses, a little like Tunis seen from the sea, with a whiff of the Mediterranean and not at all like a piece of America. But that was an illusion. It was in every sense the place where the West came to an end, the place where the frontier first got tamed."

Oskar Maurus Fontana
Austrian writer (13.4.1889–4.5.1969)
"The Fire's Breath"

"Were not the bridges alone something to wonder at . . . like the Brooklyn Bridge and the Golden Gate Bridge of Frisco? Its building of bridges was for Heinrich the most visible and most exalted triumph of the spirit of the New World and perhaps in times to come – he felt – that was the task of America, also between the peoples of the world, in their confused state of Babel, to build such bridges, swaying on gigantic cables, over enormous gulfs in origins and feelings and thoughts."

Herbert Gold
American writer
(b. 9.3.1924)

"While New York and Paris can't wait to become larger variations on Cleveland . . . San Francisco secretly remains the same."

Arthur Holitscher
Austrian writer
(22.8.1869–14.10.1941)

"For many a year my thoughts will return to the city at the Golden Gate, to the wonderful fairytale city where in a tropical garden I for the first time saw the sun setting in breathtaking splendour over the Pacific in the limitless waters of the West. San Francisco has mastered its fate and I find myself in a city that has been born anew."

Johannes V. Jensen
Danish poet
(20.1.1873–25.11.1950).
"The New World"

"Anyone who has been in Frisco retains particularly fond memories of this beautiful, bustling city, which lay as the farthermost outpost on the frontier between two worlds, pampered by the sun, apparently itself unaware of the exotic aura of golden dreams woven around its name. . . . Frisco arises anew. The best estimate is made of when to expect the next earthquake and homes are built accordingly; in the interval following every earthquake a new San Francisco is born."

Rudyard Kipling
English writer
(30.12.1865–18.1.1936)
From Sea to Sea

"A journalist asked me what I thought of the city (San Francisco) and I promptly responded that for me Bret Harte had made it hallowed ground. That was the truth . . . San

Francisco is a mad city, largely inhabited by the wholly deranged, whose women are of a remarkable beauty."

"San Francisco was a dream, a temptress of old; I knew the name, I loved the city, familiar to me since my first days as a reader. San Francisco was the ultimate Wild West, adventure itself, the haven of the prodigal son, the bank clerk on the run, the profligate and the unruly, a magnet for the bold, a new life for those that had gone astray, last hope of the poor and the oppressed . . . , for me a place where I devoutly wished to be."

Wolfgang Koeppen
German writer
(b. 23.6.1906)
"American Journey"

"How much you love or hate a city depends on what it means to you and how it treats you. I love San Francisco. To me it means many things, above all freedom. . . . I love San Francisco because for me it's full of memories. San Francisco itself is art, above all literary art, and I recall to mind, with profound respect, the great writers that were born here or came here to write: Jack London, Mark Twain, Ambrose Bierce and George Sterling. Every block is a short story, every hill a novel. Every home is a poem, every dweller within immortal. That is the whole truth."

William Saroyan
American writer
(31.8.1908–18.5.1981)

"Monsieur Verdier, owner of the great department store 'City of Paris' in San Francisco is a survivor of the earthquake and conflagration that destroyed three-quarters of the city. He was a young man at the time and retained a clear recollection of the catastrophe. He then lived through the reconstruction of the city, which in 1913 was still Asian in character, and its subsequent Americanisation. Thus he recalled three different San Franciscos. Us, we ourselves change in unchanging cities and our houses, the areas we live in, outlive us; American cities change far faster than the people who live in them and thus it is the people that outlive the cities. For us a city primarily means the past – for the American it stands first and foremost for the future and what they love about it is all that is yet to come, all that they can become."

Jean-Paul Sartre
French philosopher
(21.6.1905–15.4.1980)
Situations III

"There has never been anything to parallel San Francisco nor will there ever be. Like the magic seed of the Indian juggler that sprouted, blossomed and bore fruit before the very eyes of the onlooker so San Francisco seems in one day to have accomplished the growth of half a century."

Bayard Taylor
American writer
(11.1.1825–19.12.1878)

"Thank God I'm out of Canada again and back in the ghastly USA. Los Angeles and Hollywood are the nightmarish zenith of my crazy, lonely tour. But San Francisco! It is and has everything. . . . In Canada, five hours' flying away, you would never think that a place like San Francisco can exist. The glorious sunshine, the hills, the great bridges, the Pacific at the feet. Lovely Chinatown. Every race in the world."

Dylan Thomas
Welsh poet
(27.10.1914–9.11.1953)

"The great calamity . . . left no one with the impression that it amounted to an irrecoverable loss. This afternoon everyone is talking about it but no one is in the slightest downcast . . . Nowhere is there any doubt but that San Francisco will rise again, bigger, better and after the very briefest of intervals."

H. G. Wells
English writer
(21.9.1866–13.8.1946)
The Future in America; a Search after Realities

San Francisco from A to Z

Alcatraz Island H32

Location
1½ miles (2·5 km) NE, in the Bay of San Francisco.

Quay
Pier 41 (Fisherman's Wharf)

Ferry services
From Pier 41: Summer, daily 9.45 a.m.–4.15 p.m. (winter until 2.45 p.m.) every ½ hour.
Last boat leaves the island at 4.35 p.m. Far includes self-guided tour.

Reservation required
At Pier 41 ticket booth, or tel. 546–2882.

Even nowadays there are few tourists who neglect the opportunity of visiting the Isla de los Alcatraces ("Island of the Pelicans"). From 1933 to 1963 it was the site of the most notorious penitentiary in the United States.

The rocky island covers an area of some 12 acres (5 hectares), and the land rises to a height of 135 ft (41 m). But as there were no springs it remained uninhabited until 1853 when the first lighthouse was erected on it. Soon afterwards it was fortified, and during the Civil War (1861–5) it became a military prison. In 1933 a penitentiary for prisoners convicted of serious crimes was erected here.

In the course of its 30-year existence the penitentiary received a total of 1576 convicts. But there were never more than 250 at any one time though there were 450 cells measuring about 10 by 4 ft (3 by 1·5 m) in the building. At times the number of guards, etc., was greater than that of the convicts. After the penitentiary was closed the island was virtually forgotten for six years until it was taken over by Indians who squatted there for seven years. Although the island has been open to visitors since 1973 only emergency repairs have been made to the run-down buildings.

Alcatraz: an island penitentiary for decades then occupied by Indians

A tip: as the island is frequently shrouded in mist and the wind is almost always strong, it is a good idea to wear warm clothes when making a visit.

The Anchorage (Shopping and Pleasure Centre)   H8(H4)

The Anchorage is one of the latest attractions of San Francisco. There are nearly 50 shops and restaurants on various levels, as well as an hotel with a delightful architectural setting.
The centre of the complex is an inner courtyard where buskers from all parts of the city perform in a mini-amphitheatre.

Location
Leavenworth Street

Bus routes
15, 19, 30, 32

Cable cars
59, 60

Angel Island State Park   H32

Angel Island lies N of the city in San Francisco Bay. It has an area of 740 acres (300 hectares). In the course of the last hundred years it was used as a quarantine station for immigrants from Asia and as a coastguard station, becoming a prisoner-of-war camp and an anti-rocket site during the Second World War. The uninhabited island is now a municipal park where some 200 head of red deer are allowed to run free. Motor vehicles are banned from the island. But it is a favourite spot for excursions from the city as there are pleasant cycle tracks and paths for pedestrians as well as large picnic sites.

Location
3 miles (5 km) N on San Francisco Bay

Quay
Pier 43½ (Fisherman's Wharf)

Ferry services
To Ayala Cove; Summer: daily; Winter: weekends and holidays

One of the city's latest attractions: the Anchorage shopping centre

Part of the Bank of America complex – A. P. Gianni Plaza

Asian Art Museum of San Francisco

See Golden Gate Park

Balclutha

See National Maritime Museum

*Bank of America   I8(J5)

Address
555 California Street

This skyscraper belonging to the largest American bank is 52 storeys high and rises 778 ft (237 m). Together with the Transamerica Pyramid it has brought a fundamental change to San Francisco's townscape.

Two eminent firms of architects, Wurster, Bernardi & Emmons and Skidmore, Owings & Merrill, with Pietro Belluschi as consultant, erected the building in 1968. The material used is reddish South Dakota granite.

The complex comprises a lofty tower with offices, a low banking hall and an open piazza with a sculpture by Masa-yuki Nagare under which there is an auditorium. In all 7500 persons work in this building. Visitors and employees are carried to the top of the tower by 32 lifts. From the highest storey there is a magnificent view.

Old and New in delightful harmony – the head office of the Bank of California

The Carnelian Room restaurant is up here. To reserve a table phone 433–7500 after 3 p.m.

Bank of California

I8(J4/5)

The Bank of California is the oldest bank on the West coast. Its buildings in San Francisco have always been distinguished for their artistic merit.

Address
400 California Street

The first bank building, which was erected here in 1867 on the site occupied by the present Banking Temple, was in the Neo-Renaissance style. It was pulled down just before the earthquake of 1906. The second head office, at the corner of Sansome Street, takes the form of a Corinthian temple. Pillars carved out of Californian granite stand on two sides of the building. Rising alongside it, at 420 California Street, is the bank's latest head office. Great importance was attached to preserving the earlier building when the new one was erected in 1967.

The "Banking Temple" not only houses the "Museum of Money of the American West" (see below) in its lower storey but also has an entrance hall whose dimensions (111 by 82 by 60 ft – 34 by 25 by 18 m) never fail to impress visitors as they come in.

Marble from Tennessee was used. At one end there are statues of two mountain lions by the Californian sculptor Arthur Putnam.

Museum of Money of the American West

Address
420 California Street

Opening times
Mon.–Thurs. 10 a.m.–
3 p.m.; Fri. 10 a.m.–5 p.m.

Closed
Public holidays

Entry free

The Museum of Money of the American West is not very large but it is an important source of information about the history of the American West. Here may be seen gold quartz from the time of the Gold Rush, and nuggets of gold and silver. There is also a collection of gold coins and banknotes dating from the second half of the 19th c. Some are official issue; others were produced by the banks themselves to cope with the shortage of coin at that period.

The interesting collections of the museum also include weapons which are historically important, some of them having been used in duels by famous personalities of the past.

*Berkeley   131

Location
12 miles (20 km) NE
(Highway 80)

Underground station
BART (to Berkeley)

Berkeley lies 12 miles NE of San Francisco. It is a town with only 140,000 inhabitants, and in spite of the large amount of industry there and the 45,000 students it has kept its character as a small town. The sights of the town are the Charles Lee Tilden Regional Park and Bancroft Way with the places of amusement and shops frequented by the students.

The main attraction, however, is the world-famous University of California. An excursion to Berkeley allows visitors to appreciate the quite unusual atmosphere of the campus of an American university. An additional attraction is the University Art Museum with a collection of paintings by artists of the 19th and 20th c., as well as an important film archive.

University of California

Address
Telegraph Avenue and
Bancroft Way

Guided tours
Mon., Wed. and Fri. at
10 a.m. Meet at Students'
Union (Visitors' Center).
Booking essential for
groups of more than 5
(tel. 642–5215)

The University of California oversees teaching in nine Californian cities. It has, after the State University of New York, the largest network of State higher educational establishments. Berkeley Campus was founded in 1873 as a private college. It is the oldest college in California and with 45,000 students it is the second largest, after Los Angeles.

The University of California is world famous not only on account of its many Nobel Prize winners. It is also remembered that it was here that the student troubles of the 1960s began, spreading all over the Western World in 1968.

Sather Tower (campanile)

Opening times
Daily 10 a.m.–4.15 p.m.

The symbol of the university is Sather Tower, a campanile built in 1914. It is modelled on the tower of St Mark's in Venice. It is over 300 ft (94 m) high and dominates all the other buildings of this extensive park-like campus. From the top (lift) there is a splendid view out over the university buildings, San Francisco Bay and the Golden Gate Bridge (see entry). The carillon merits special mention.

Other buildings

South Hall, built in 1873 in Tudor style, stands SW of the campanile. It is the oldest building on the campus. Yet farther SW is Sather Gate which, with the Plaza, is the centre of student life here.

Sather Tower – the symbol of the University of California at Berkeley ▶

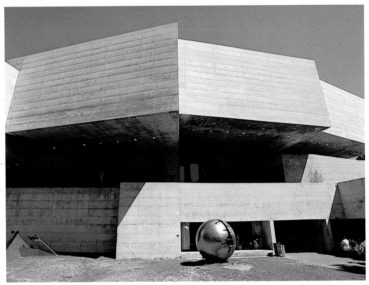

Berkeley – the modern façade of Berkeley University Art Museum . . .

The Earth Sciences Building, not far from the North Tower, houses palaeontological and mineralogical collections as well an interesting seismograph on the first floor.

In the Chapel of the Pacific School of Religion, 1198 Scenic Avenue, is one of the biggest stained-glass windows in the world. The chapel is open to visitors Mondays to Fridays from 8.30 a.m. to 4.30 p.m.

Also noteworthy is the cyclotron (particle accelerator) to the NE, and to the SE the California Memorial Stadium, a sports arena seating 76,500.

Lawrence-Berkeley Laboratory

A particularly interesting sight is the Lawrence-Berkeley Laboratory where Nobel laureate Ernest O. Lawrence carried out his pioneering research in the field of atomic physics. Among those who worked there with him was Robert Oppenheimer. He did important basic research leading to the development of the first atomic bomb. When Oppenheimer opposed the making of the hydrogen bomb an investigation was begun in 1953 into his alleged Communist tendencies. President Eisenhower refused to permit him to participate any longer in secret projects.

It is possible to take a conducted tour around these most interesting research installations, but only on Tuesdays at 2 p.m. (except on public holidays and during the summer vacation). Application must be made in advance by telephone (tel. 843–2740, extension 5611).

Museums

As well as the University Art Museum the following campus museums deserve mention.

. . . and a view of the exhibition galleries, a delightful example of modern architecture

The Judah L. Magnes Memorial Museum, 2911 Russell Street, is mainly devoted to a collection of Jewish ritual objects. Two libraries are associated with the museum. (Open Sundays to Fridays from 10 a.m. to 4 p.m.)

The Palestine Institute has displays of archaeological finds from Palestine, dating from Old Testament times to the 5th c. A.D. (Open daily from 9 a.m. to 5 p.m.)

In the Robert H. Lowie Museum of Anthropology visitors can examine the anthropological exhibits. (Open Mondays to Fridays from 10 a.m. to 4 p.m., and Saturdays and Sundays from noon to 4 p.m.)

University Art Museum

This museum on the university campus was built in 1970 to designs by Mario Ciampi. It has already won renown during its few years of existence. Its own collections are considerably larger than might be expected in a museum founded so recently. The explanation is that the university itself became active in the collecting field soon after its foundation in 1873 and handed over to the new museum what it had already acquired. It was Hans Hofmann, a German painter active in America from 1932 onwards, who provided the decisive impetus to plans to build a museum here. He had taught for a while at Berkeley, and in 1963 he presented the university with 45 of his paintings and also

Address
2626 Bancroft Way

Opening times
Wed.–Sun. 11 a.m.–5 p.m.

37

promised to provide funds for a museum. Seven years later the buildings were ready. Nowadays about half of the works Hofmann gave to the museum are on show in one of the largest galleries. There is accordingly no better place to gain a general impression of this painter's work. Among Hofmann's American pupils were Louise Nevelson, Helen Frankenthaler and Larry Rivers.

The Museum also possesses a large collection of Oriental works of art and many 19th c. paintings. There are almost always several special exhibitions on here at any time. They are usually devoted primarily to the work of 20th c. painters, sculptors and photographers.

Pacific Film Archive

The museum also houses the Pacific Film Archive. There are always interesting series of film shows running in its 200-seat auditorium. It has a stock of 5000 movies, including the largest number of Japanese movies outside Japan itself. It also has many *avant-garde* and experimental US movies and a collection of 35 mm copies of Soviet silent movies. Film shows daily 7–11 p.m.; (programme and information tel. 642 1124).

Buddha's Universal Church

See Chinatown

**Cable Cars   H–K 3–6

San Francisco is built on several hills. A major contribution to the development of the city was made by the invention of the cable cars in 1873. Since 1964 these tram-like vehicles have enjoyed the unique distinction of being the only public transport system which has been declared an historic monument.

Andrew Hallidie was an Englishman who came to California at the time of the Gold Rush. He made steel cables for mining. At this period all transport was horse drawn. When in 1869 Hallidie witnessed a serious traffic accident caused by a horse losing its footing on a slippery road, he conceived the idea of replacing the horse trams with a more modern transport system. After three years' experiment he succeeded, and on 2 August 1873 he demonstrated the first car in Clay Street.

His invention consisted in making use of a cable housed in a trench under the street and kept moving by enormous wheels in specially constructed engine houses ("barns"). The "gripmen", as the drivers are called, had to place the vehicles in position on the travelling cables and lock them on so that they were held fast. This made it possible to cope with even the city's steepest hills. In 1890 there were no fewer than eight companies running cable car services. They had in all more than 600 vehicles and a network of more than 100 miles (160 km).

Today there remain no more than 37 vehicles on three lines. The network embraces just 12 miles (19 km), which is covered at the steady speed of 9½ m.p.h. Of the old barns only one remains.

The cable cars – they cope with the city's steepest hills

The Cable Car Barn – control centre for the cable cars

Cable Cars

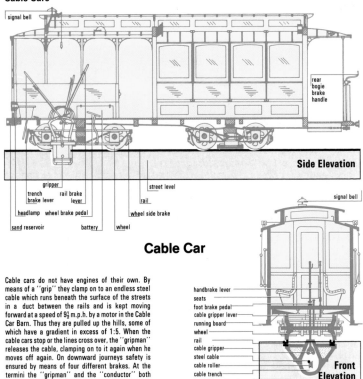

Side Elevation

signal bell

rear bogie brake handle

gripper
trench brake lever · rail brake lever
street level
headlamp · wheel brake pedal
rail
signal bell
sand reservoir · battery · wheel
wheel side brake

Cable Car

Cable cars do not have engines of their own. By means of a "grip" they clamp on to an endless steel cable which runs beneath the surface of the streets in a duct between the rails and is kept moving forward at a speed of 9½ m.p.h. by a motor in the Cable Car Barn. Thus they are pulled up the hills, some of which have a gradient in excess of 1:5. When the cable cars stop or the lines cross over, the "gripman" releases the cable, clamping on to it again when he moves off again. On downward journeys safety is ensured by means of four different brakes. At the termini the "gripman" and the "conductor" both have to turn the car about on a turntable.

handbrake lever
seats
foot brake pedal
cable gripper lever
running board
wheel
rail
cable gripper
steel cable
cable roller
cable trench
foundations of road

Front Elevation

Most of the vehicles still in service date from the last century. Built of wood, they seat 30–34 passengers, but there are generally another 50 standing or strap-hanging.

In spite of numerous accidents the cable cars remain very dear to the people of San Francisco. The constitution of the city contains a clause forbidding the discontinuance of the service. From October 1982 to June 1984 the service of cable cars was suspended, so that the long-due general overhaul of the network and the cars themselves could be undertaken. The cost of renovation amounted to 63·5 million dollars, of which all but 12 million came from the State.

Cable Car Museum

14

Address
Corner of Washington Street and Mason Street

Opening times
May–Sept, daily
10 a.m.–6 p.m.; Oct.–Apr.,
daily 10 a.m.–5 p.m.

This red-brick building was erected in 1887 as the control centre for the three cable car lines still in existence. From an observation gallery it is possible to see just how the cable cars work. Since their invention in 1873 the system has remained essentially unchanged.

In the museum visitors can examine three of the earliest

vehicles which plied in Clay Street as well as photographs and models of all the types of cable car ever put into service. Continuous screening of a film lasting a quarter of an hour about the cable cars and how they operate.

Closed
Thanksgiving Day, Christmas Day and New Year's Day

Entry free

California Academy of Sciences (Museum)

See Golden Gate Park

California Historical Society (Museum)   G8

The California Historical Society is housed in Whittier Mansion, the residence which a well-to-do merchant had built in 1896. It does not only maintain contemporary interiors which give us an idea of the extravagant *fin-de-siècle* life style of the richest inhabitants of San Francisco but also possesses a comprehensive collection of lithographs, watercolours, oil paintings and drawings relating to the history of San Francisco and California up to about 1906. This collection is shown in exhibitions that are regularly changed.
The Library of the Society is situated just round the corner at 2099 Pacific Avenue. It has one of the most important collections of books, periodicals, photographs, etc., relating to the history of the city and the State (tel. 567–1848 for schedule).

Address
2090 Jackson Street

Bus route
2 (to Laguna Street)

Opening times
Tues.–Sun. 1–4 p.m.

Conducted tours
Tues.–Sun. 1.30 p.m. (also 3 p.m. at weekends)

Entrance fee charged
(Free on 1st Wed. of month)

*California Palace of the Legion of Honor (Museum)   B9

There is no other museum outside France which has so comprehensive a collection of French art as the California Palace of the Legion of Honor on the extreme NW outskirts of San Francisco. The Neo-Classical museum building which is in a most picturesque situation on a hillock in Lincoln Park is a copy of the Palais de la Légion d'Honneur in Paris. It was a gift from the German American Adolph B. Spreckels and his wife, *née* Alma Bretteville.
The California Palace of the Legion of Honor is unique among American museums in being devoted exclusively to French art. This was indeed the plan at the time of its inauguration in 1924, but in the course of the years works by artists from other lands were acquired. When, in 1972, the California Palace was combined with the De Young Museum (see Golden Gate Park) by administrative decree in order to save expense – for both museums are controlled by the city – the works that were not French were transferred to the De Young Museum which for its part handed over all its French collections to the California Palace.
Despite its rather out-of-the-way situation, the museum attracts some 300,000 visitors every year. The museum has three munificent families to thank for most of its collections.

Location
Lincoln Park

Bus routes
2, 38

Opening times
Wed.–Sun. 10 a.m.–5 p.m.

Entrance fee charged
(Free 1st Wed. of month)
Sat. entrance free between 10 a.m. and noon.
Fee also admits you to M. H. de Young Memorial Museum and Asian Art Museum on the same day.

41

California Palace of the Legion of Honor

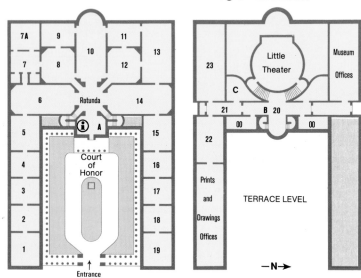

Rooms 1-3	French Middle Ages and Renaissance	
Room 4	School of Fontainebleau	
Room 5	French Baroque	
Room 6	Age of Louis XV	
Room 7	French Rococo	
Room 7A	French 18th c.	
Rooms 8, 10, 12	Rodin and his contemporaries	
Room 9	18th c.	
Room 11	Temporary Exhibitions	

Rooms 13 and 14	19th c.
Rooms 15–20	Temporary Exhibitions
Rooms 21 and 22	Prints, Graphics (Achenbach Foundation) Temporary Exhibitions
Room 23	Porcelain
A	Bookstall
B	Telephone
C	Café Chanticleer
00	Toilets
(i)	Information

Gifts

The Spreckels family collected mainly 18th c. works as well as original bronze castings by Rodin, whose "Thinker" stands in the Court of Honor in front of the museum.

Mr and Mrs Archer B. Huntington bequeathed furniture, tapestries and a number of paintings.

Mr and Mrs H. K. S. Williams not only gave the museum in 1944 a comprehensive collection of French art but also made available a large sum of money for the purchase of works from France.

Collections

To give a detailed account of the collections of the California Palace of the Legion of Honor would take us beyond the limits of this book. The plan of the building provides some idea of what is here. The fact that there is no equally comprehensive display of French art outside France has been emphasised even further after a reorganisation of the galleries in 1979–80, because there has been since then a permanent exhibition here called "The French Legacy". In it the most important works in the museum have been brought together, including an Angers tapestry dating

California Palace of the Legion of Honor – devoted exclusively to French art

from 1380. A complete 18th c. interior from the "Hotel d'Humières" in Paris deserves special attention.

With these will be found also works by the most important French painters – Claude Lorrain, Nicolas Poussin, Georges de La Tour, François Boucher, Jean Honoré Fragonard, Jean-Antoine Watteau, Louis David, Camille Corot, Gustave Courbet, Edgar Degas, Edouard Manet, Claude Monet and many others.

The Achenbach Foundation for Graphic Arts constitutes a further attraction of the California Palace. It is a collection of graphic works amounting to more than 100,000 sheets dating from the 15th c. to the 20th c. Mr Moore Achenbach and his wife Sadie presented it to the city, and at their wish it was housed here. Valuable illustrated books as well as a library of some 3000 volumes relative to the graphic arts form part of this collection.

Achenbach Foundation for Graphic Arts

---

*The Cannery (Shopping and Leisure Centre)   H7

On the S side of Fisherman's Wharf (see entry) an interesting complex with fashion houses, food shops, boutiques, art galleries, cafés and restaurants has developed since 1967 on the premises, now nearly a hundred years old, of the redundant Del Monte fruit canning factory. There are similar developments at Ghirardelli Square and Pier 39 (see entries). Open-air concerts, poetry readings and other shows are put on here.

Address
2801 Leavenworth Street
(near Fisherman's Wharf)

Bus routes
15, 19, 30

Cable cars
59, 60

The Cannery – a centre for shopping and leisure

Carmel – Old World nostalgia in present-day America

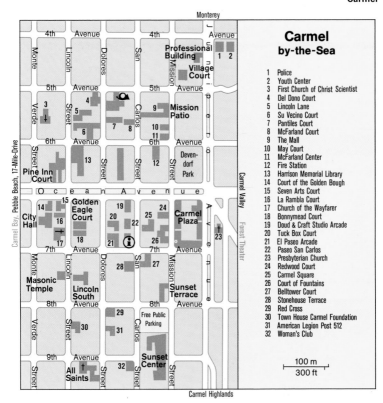

Monterey

Carmel
by-the-Sea

1 Police
2 Youth Center
3 First Church of Christ Scientist
4 Del Dono Court
5 Lincoln Lane
6 Su Vecino Court
7 Pantiles Court
8 McFarland Court
9 The Mall
10 May Court
11 McFarland Center
12 Fire Station
13 Harrison Memorial Library
14 Court of the Golden Bough
15 Seven Arts Court
16 La Rambla Court
17 Church of the Wayfarer
18 Bonnymead Court
19 Doud & Craft Studio Arcade
20 Tuck Box Court
21 El Paseo Arcade
22 Paseo San Carlos
23 Presbyterian Church
24 Redwood Court
25 Carmel Square
26 Court of Fountains
27 Belltower Court
28 Stonehouse Terrace
29 Red Cross
30 Town House Carmel Foundation
31 American Legion Post 512
32 Woman's Club

100 m
300 ft

Carmel Highlands

At the same time this complex bears witness to the efforts for urban renewal being made by San Francisco architects. Musicians and entertainers perform in an inner courtyard where the olive trees are almost a hundred years old. There is a noteworthy Byzantine mosaic ceiling in Cannery Casuals on the third floor. From the Cannery there is also a splendid view of the harbour.

Opening times
Mon.–Sat. 10 a.m.–6 p.m.;
Sun. 11 a.m.–6 p.m.
Summer: open to 9 p.m.
daily (Restaurants to midnight)

*Carmel

For many travellers Monterey (see entry) is no more than a stopping point on the way to Carmel, which really no visitor to California should miss. Thanks to its narrow streets, its village architecture in which English influence is obvious and its peaceful atmosphere, except at weekends when the village is inundated with visitors, Carmel has a particular charm all its own.

Carmel's shops, restaurants and hotels have a special

Location
106 miles S (170 km).
117 miles (188 km) via
17 Mile Drive

45

character and a certain Old World charm. It is an unusual place because no house, not even a shop front, can be put up without permission from the local authority and no tree can be felled without an official permit. In Carmel there are few sidewalks, the houses are not numbered (the Carmelites, as they are called, are expected to go and collect their own mail), and even the street lamps have a style of their own.

Carmel has attracted many artists, but the place does not have a Bohemian atmosphere, even though there are many galleries in which contemporary painters and sculptors exhibit their work. Every year in July there is a Bach festival which draws large audiences.

In stark contrast to its size – Carmel has only about 5000 permanent inhabitants – the village has a disproportionately large number of hotels, motels and restaurants. Quail Lodge (8205 Valley Greens Drive) is perhaps one of the most luxurious hotels in California with its 270 acre park, lakes, meadows, woods, a large golf course, four tennis courts and two swimming pools. Carmel has recovered from the consequence of a severe storm in 1982, although the beach has still not regained its former size.

San Carlos Borromeo del Rio Carmelo (Franciscan Mission)

Opening times
Daily 9 a.m.–5 p.m.

In Carmel stands San Carlos Borromeo del Rio Carmelo, dating from 1770. It is the second oldest of the 21 missions founded in California by the Franciscans. In fact, however, the mission was originally situated on the coast and was subsequently moved some 5 miles (8 km) inland (3080 Rio Road). In 1784 Father Junípero Serra died here at the age of 71; he it was who founded the first nine missions, from San Diego (1769) to San Buenaventura in Ventura (1782). In the church belonging to the mission there is a wooden statue of the Virgin which Serra brought here from Mexico.

Chinatown (district in San Francisco)   I8(I/J4/5)

Location
Grant Avenue (main axis)
between Columbus
Avenue and Bush Street

Conducted tours
Ding How Tours
tel. 981–8399

Chinatown is like a town within the city. The largest Chinese city outside Asia is in San Francisco. About 85,000 Chinese live on Grant Avenue between Bush Street and Columbus Avenue and in the side streets around here. This is where they have their shops, restaurants and institutions.

From 1850 onwards, that is to say, from just after the Gold Rush, Grant Street, then still called the Calle del Fundacion and the oldest street in San Francisco, began to be settled by Chinese. It was almost totally destroyed in the 1906 earthquake, but Chinatown was rebuilt entirely in Chinese style and was soon more attractive than before the disaster. Now with its temples, theatres, workshops, small businesses, stores, antique and souvenir shops, teahouses and pharmacies with their odd nostrums, Chinatown has become one of the major sights of San Francisco.

With ever-increasing immigration from Asia, Chinatown has experienced its great period of population growth in the last 30 years. Since 1950 the Chinese population has grown from 30,000 to 85,000, which means that more than a tenth of San Francisco's population is now of Chinese extraction. About one-fifth of the houses in Chinatown now belong to Chinese.

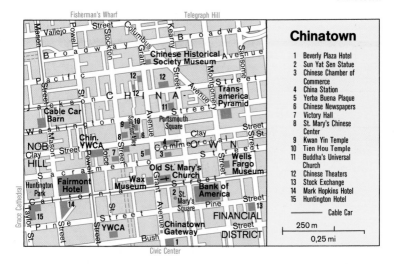

Chinatown

1 Beverly Plaza Hotel
2 Sun Yat Sen Statue
3 Chinese Chamber of
   Commerce
4 China Station
5 Yerba Buena Plaque
6 Chinese Newspapers
7 Victory Hall
8 St. Mary's Chinese
   Center
9 Kwan Yin Temple
10 Tien Hou Temple
11 Buddha's Universal
   Church
12 Chinese Theaters
13 Stock Exchange
14 Mark Hopkins Hotel
15 Huntington Hotel

——————— Cable Car

250 m

0,25 mi

A stroll around Chinatown

A stroll through Chinatown ought to start at Chinatown Gateway, on the corner of Grant Avenue and Bush Street. It was erected in 1970 and is a gate of characteristic Oriental construction, decorated with dragons and other beasts. Though Grant Avenue up to Bush Street was widened in the 19th c. like most other thoroughfares in San Francisco, the street as it runs away beyond Chinatown Gate gives the best impression of what the city must once have looked like.

Chinatown Gateway

Old St Mary's Church (on the corner of Grant Avenue and California Street) is the oldest Catholic church in San Francisco. It was built in 1854 and badly damaged in the 1906 earthquake and by a serious fire 60 years later. Today, however, it has been restored to the appearance it had in the early days of San Francisco. Originally a cathedral, it is now simply a parish church. The new St Mary's Cathedral (see entry) is on Cathedral Hill. Above the clock dial is carved the admonition: "Son Observe the Time and Fly from Evil". Apart from the church the clergy house is worthy of attention. It was built in 1964 to the designs of the New York architects Skidmore, Owings & Merrill. (Open daily 9 a.m.–8 p.m.)

Old St Mary's Church

From Old St Mary's Church there is a view of St Mary's Square. The site was presented to the city by the Catholic diocese in 1912. Today there is an underground garage here. On the square stands Beniamino Bufano's statue of Dr Sun Yat-sen, the first president of the Republic of China (1 January 1912–14 February 1912). Early in the 20th c. he spent several years of political asylum in San Francisco.

St Mary's Square

Tin How Temple, named for the Buddhist Queen of Heaven

Opposite Old St Mary's Church is the Chinatown Wax Museum with groups illustrating the Chinese in American history (601 Grant Avenue, open daily 10 a.m.–11 p.m.).
A little to the N of Old St Mary's Church there is a remarkable telephone kiosk in the Chinese style.

Chinatown Wax Museum

The noteworthy building of the Soo Yuen Benevolent Institution on the corner of Grant Avenue and Clay Street was given its Chinese appearance only in 1912.

Soo Yuen Benevolent Institution

San Francisco began its existence at the spot where Dick Young House (823 Grant Avenue) now stands between Clay Street and Washington Street.
On this spot on 25 June 1835 the first human habitation of Yerba Buena, as San Francisco was originally called, was erected. In fact it was a tent which was replaced by the first timber house a few months later. A plaque has been fixed to the wall of Dick Young House to commemorate the event.

Dick Young House

Tien How Temple is on the top floor of 125 Waverly Place (between Washington and Clay Streets). It is relatively easy for non-Buddhists to visit the temple. The temple was founded in 1852 on another site; it bears the name of Tien How, the Buddhist Queen of Heaven (open daily 10 a.m.–4 p.m.)

Tien How Temple

This building was erected only in 1977 on the corner of Clay Street and Stockton Street. It is the head office of the oldest

Kong Chow Benevolent Association and Temple

◀ *Old St Mary's Church – San Francisco's oldest Catholic church is in Chinatown*

Bank of Canton: styled right for Chinatown

Chinese friendly society in America, the Kong Chow Benevolent Association. Visiting times for the temple (situated on the third floor), which bears the same name, are 9 a.m. to 4 p.m. daily.
The central post office for Chinatown is on the ground floor.

Chinese Six Companies

The headquarters of the Chinese Six Companies (843 Stockton Street) is perhaps the most important institution in Chinatown. In the 19th c. it recruited Chinese labourers, the so-called Coolies (the word itself means roughly "hard labour"), to build the Transcontinental Railway. Later it functioned as a sort of arbitrator to sort out quarrels between Chinese. Today it has lost something of its former prestige, but is still of considerable social significance.

Bank of Canton

The building like a pagoda on the corner of Grant Avenue and Washington Street is at present occupied by the Bank of Canton. It was built in 1909 as the Chinatown telephone office. From 1894 to 1949 there was a Chinese language telephone service which operated independently of the central San Francisco exchange; calls were put through manually. In 1847 the first San Francisco newspaper, the "California Star" was printed here.

Spofford Alley

Spofford Alley turns off between Clay Street and Washington Street. It is one of those interesting alleys of the sort that can hardly be seen outside Chinatown. Beyond Washington Street it joins Old Chinatown Lane, once notorious for its many brothels and gambling halls.

The Fidelity Savings Bank, at 845 Grant Avenue, near Washington Street, was built in 1971. It is in the most extravagant modern Chinese style. The roof is covered with gilded tiles.

Fidelity Savings Bank

Buddha's Universal Church, the largest Buddhist temple in America, was built in 1961 on the corner of Washington Street and Kearny Street by members of the Pristine Orthodox Dharma, a strongly Americanised modern offshoot of Buddhism. On the roof may be seen in addition to a lotus pool a Bodhi tree, said to be a shoot from the tree under which the Buddha more than 2500 years ago arrived at enlightenment (Bodhi). Open the second and fourth Sunday of the month (February to November only) 1 p.m. to 2.30 p.m. Tours possible if arranged in advance (tel. 982–6116).

Buddha's Universal Church

This museum devoted to the history of the Chinese in America is to be found at 650 Commercial Street. The collections are primarily of objects, photographs and documents relative to the role of the Chinese during the Californian Gold Rush. The museum also has, however, important material about later periods. Every exhibit is labelled in Chinese and English.
The museum is open Tuesday to Saturday from 1 p.m. to 5 p.m. It is closed on public holidays. Free entry.

Chinese Historical Society of America Museum

In and around John Street there are three Chinese theatres. A visit is particularly interesting because of the simple style of staging, the dissonant music, the exotic audience, the wonderful costumes and the apparent lack of event in the plots of the plays, the performance of which used to go on for days on end and in which formerly even the women's roles were taken by men (see Practical Information – Theatres).

Theatres

See Practical Information – Restaurants.

Restaurants

Chinese Culture Center

I8(J4)

The Chinese Culture Center came into existence when Holiday Inn Hotel was built. It occupies its second floor. It is primarily a meeting place for San Francisco's Chinese. In the auditorium, which forms part of it and seats 450, there are often cultural, political and religious events.
The Culture Center also serves as a museum where Chinese works of art are displayed and other branches of Chinese culture are practised. Entry free.

Address
750 Kearny Street

Opening times
Tues.–Sat. 10 a.m.–4 p.m.

Closed
Sun., Mon. and public holidays

City Hall

See Civic Center

*Civic Center (Official and Administrative Centre)

H9(H6)

No other city in America has such a magnificent official and administrative centre as San Francisco. Its focal point is Civic Center Plaza, a quadrilateral square around which are

Location
Market Street, Van Ness Av, Golden Gate triangle

The Civic Center, San Francisco's Official and Administrative Centre

Bus routes
5, 31

grouped the various buildings – the vast City Hall, the Louise M. Davies Symphony Hall, the War Memorial Opera House, the Ballet Building, Herbst Theater, the San Francisco Museum of Modern Art (in the War Memorial Veteran's Building), the Civic Auditorium, the Main Public Library, the Federal Building, the Federal Office Building, the State Office Building, etc., and beneath the Civic Center Plaza – the Brooks Exhibit Hall.

City Hall

Opening times
During office hours

Guided tours
Thurs. – noon
Meet at History Room in
Main Public Library

On the W side of the square stands the 300 ft (92 m) high City Hall. It is the fifth City Hall that San Francisco has had; the fourth, was on the site now occupied by the Main Public Library, collapsed during the 1906 earthquake before construction was completed. The present building was constructed between 1912 and 1915 to designs by two Californian architects, John Bakewell and Arthur Brown jr. They conceived a building on the lines of a French Renaissance château. It is nearly 400 ft (122 m) long and 300 ft (92 m) wide. Its offices are round an enclosed courtyard over which a dome has been placed. It is 300 ft (92 m) high, a few metres higher than even the Capitol in Washington. The drum which is surrounded by pillars reaches a height of 190 ft (58 m); the diameter of the dome is just 85 ft (26 m) at this point. The City Hall contains the offices of the city's administration including the mayor's office, council chambers of the Board of Supervisors, and city courts. The building reflects the municipal pride of the citizens of San Francisco.

Two of the many public buildings in the Civic Center – the City Hall . . .

. . . and the War Memorial Opera House

Main Public Library

Information
Tel. 558–3949

The Main Public Library, the headquarters of the city's library services, is on the E side of the square, opposite the City Hall. The building was constructed in 1917 by George Kelham in Beaux-Arts style; the steel magnate Andrew Carnegie provided munificent financial support. The library has a stock of some 1·2 million books, not to mention a considerable collection of newspapers and manuscripts (temporary exhibitions on the 2nd and 3rd floors). The building became too small for all its functions long ago.

A city library was founded in San Francisco as long ago as 1879. It first occupied rented rooms in Bush Street and began to loan out books in 1880. The present Main Public Library, which supports 26 branches throughout San Francisco, stands where in 1906 the fourth City Hall collapsed before it was completed. Earlier still the cemetery of Yerba Buena (as San Francisco was originally called) occupied this site. Two further items of interest are the monumental murals by Frank DuMond in the reading and catalogue room; they depict scenes from pioneering days in California.

Open
Tues. and Fri. noon–6 p.m.,
Wed. 1 p.m.–6 p.m., Thurs.
and Sat. 10 a.m.–6 p.m.

Entry free

On the second floor is the San Francisco History Room. Here are old books, newspapers, maps, photographs and other documents, plus household items salvaged from the 1906 earthquake and displays of the San Francisco Police Department. The Old Federal Building is behind Main Public Library.

Civic Auditorium (Conference Centre)

The Civic Auditorium, the oldest building in the Civic Center, stands on the S side of Civic Center Plaza. It now serves together with Brooks Exhibit Hall, which was constructed alongside in 1958, as the city's conference centre. The Civic Auditorium itself seats 7000 people and was built in 1915 for the great Panama-Pacific Exhibition. The architect was Arthur Brown jr. who was also responsible for the plans of the City Hall, the War Memorial Opera House and the Veteran's Building.

*San Francisco Museum of Modern Art

Opening times
Tues., Wed., Fri. 10 a.m.–
5 p.m.; Thurs. 10 a.m.–
9 p.m.; Sat., Sun. 11 a.m.–
5 p.m.

Closed
Mon. and public holidays

Entrance fee charged
(Free on 1st Tues. of
month. Half-price Thurs.
after 5 p.m.)

The San Francisco Museum of Modern Art is housed in the War Memorial Veteran's Building on the W side of Civic Center Plaza. This museum received its present name only in 1976; before then it was simply called the San Francisco Museum of Art. It is a private institution, unlike the three other major art museums in San Francisco, the Asia Art Museum in Golden Gate Park, the California Palace of the Legion of Honor and the M. H. de Young Memorial Museum in Golden Gate Park (see entries). Its origins go back to the 1890s, but it was set on a firm footing only in 1916 thanks to the efforts of the San Francisco Art Association.

The museum was originally housed in the Palace of Fine Arts constructed in the Presidio for the Panama-Pacific Exhibition, where the Exploratorium is now to be found. It left these premises which were gradually falling into disrepair and had to put its collections into store for ten years until it

Façade of the San Francisco Museum of Modern Art

Sculptures by Jackson Pollock, Robert Hudson and Manuel Neri

"House of Cards" (1959/60) by the American artist Al Held

The avant-garde *artist Frank Stella's "Khurasan Gate" (1969)*

was offered a floor of the War Memorial Veterans Building which belonged to the city. It has occupied these premises since 1935. They were not purpose built and though it has also taken over another floor and a store in the basement it is seriously short of space because the collections have been growing all the time.

San Francisco Museum of Modern Art was the only museum of its type on the West Coast until a museum of modern art was opened in Los Angeles in 1986. This gave the San Francisco museum particular importance.

As well as the permanent collection there are frequent major exhibitions which up to now have generally been organised by other American museums. The San Francisco Museum is, however, increasingly taking responsibility for its own exhibitions and sending out touring exhibitions to other cities.

It is only recently that it has been obvious even from the outside that this is a museum devoted exclusively to the art of the 20th c. Works by the American sculptors Tony Smith and Peter Voulkos have been placed in front of the building the Art Deco façade of which, it must be admitted, does not give an up-to-date impression. Modernisation has also had its effect on the entrance hall. The statue of George Washington, paid for by the Daughters of the American Revolution, a patriotic league, has been swept away and replaced by a geometric object made of steel by the Californian sculptor Bruce Nauman. The impression that the museum is gradually changing its image is strengthened even by the ultra-modern museum shop on the ground floor. It is well stocked with books on art and photography, posters, etc. The management has hopes of taking over the whole building one day.

Understandably Californian artists who are not generally well known are singled out for attention, especially those American painters and sculptors who have made the West Coast their cultural home, such as Mark Rothko, Clyfford Still, Robert Motherwell, Jackson Pollock, Philip Guston and Sam Francis. Still, who died in 1981, presented the museum with 28 of his large-scale abstract paintings, and Guston gave several works to the museum before his death in 1980. Negotiations are in train with Motherwell and Francis. Richard Diebenkorn, an internationally renowned Californian painter, has already made major gifts.

The permanent collections of the museum now contain works by nearly every important modern European or American artist. But as regards European art there can be no comparison with the Museum of Modern Art in New York either in quantity or quality.

Henri Matisse is especially well represented with nine paintings. George Braque's wonderful masterpiece "Le Guéridon" is also on show. In 1980 the Josef Albers collection was greatly enhanced by the gift of seven more works. Among the German artists represented here are Max Ernst, George Grosz, Hans Hartung, Karl Hoer, Ernst Ludwig Kirchner, Franz Marc, Max Pechstein, Hans Purrmann, Kurt Schwitters and Fritz Winter. There are works by the Russian artists Alexej Jawlensky and Wassily Kandinsky. As for the French, the most impressive are Pierre Bonnard, Paul Cézanne, Jean Dubuffet, Fernand Léger, Camille Pissarro

20th c. Art

20th c. West Coast art

Art from Europe and the USA

Louise M. Davies Symphony Hall – San Francisco's ultra-modern concert hall

and Georges Rouault. There are also works by the Spanish artists Joan Miró and Pablo Picasso.

The museum possesses works by the following sculptors: Alexander Archipenko, Hans Arp, Constantin Brâncusi, Jacob Epstein, Henri Laurens, Jacques Lipchitz, Marino Marini and Henry Moore.

Sculptures

As well as the American artists mentioned above, the museum exhibits works by others who have aroused public interest during the last decades, including Stuart Davis, Jim Dine, Helen Frankenthaler, Arshile Gorky, Adolph Gottlieb, Robert Indiana, Elsworth Kelly, William de Kooning, Kenneth Noland, Georgia O'Keeffe, Claes Oldenburg, Ad Reinhardt, Frank Stella and Mark Tobey.

Avant-garde

The museum also has a large collection of photographs. Especially noteworthy are the several hundred original prints of pictures by Ansel Adams, a photographer who died in 1984.

Photograph collection

War Memorial Opera House

The War Memorial Opera House stands just S of the San Francisco Museum of Modern Art. It was built in 1932 by Arthur Brown jr. together with the Veteran's Building opposite the City Hall. Up until 1980 performances were given here by both the San Francisco Opera (founded in 1923) and the San Francisco Symphony. Consequently their respective seasons could only be short. Now, however, the Symphony Orchestra is able to use the recently built Louise M.

◄ *Tom Holland's "McAdoo" (1981)*

59

Victorian façades in Cow Hollow

Davies Symphony Hall. The War Memorial Opera House is also home to the San Francisco Ballet.

The United Nations was inaugurated in the War Memorial Opera House and the Veteran's Building. The Charter founding the international parliament was signed by representatives of 43 nations on the stage of the Opera House on 26 June 1945. This event is commemorated by United Nations Plaza, a square at the E end of the Civic Center.

*Louise M. Davies Symphony Hall

The opening of this concert hall in September 1980 was the fulfilment of a long-cherished ambition of music-lovers in San Francisco: at last the Symphony Orchestra, which hitherto had had to share the Memorial Opera House with the Opera and the Ballet, had a home of its own.

The building was designed by the New York firm of architects Skidmore, Owings & Merrill, with the collaboration of Pietro Belluschi. It had to fit in with the rest of the Civic Center but be modern in conception. There was no question of imitating the Art Deco style chosen for the other buildings. Therefore both internally and externally the building represents a compromise between old and new, tradition and modernity. Yet taken as a whole it must be regarded as one of the most interesting new buildings in San Francisco. Though it has seating for 3000, it has an intimate feel about it. The acoustic problems which immediately became obvious have since been overcome, so that San Francisco can

The Embarcadero Center, one of the most original examples of urban renewal

look with pride on this concert hall which was financed entirely out of private resources.

Coit Tower

See Telegraph Hill

Conservatory of Flowers

See Golden Gate Park

Cow Hollow (District)

G8

In the years following the Gold Rush the part of present-day Union Street W of Van Ness Avenue was a green valley. People used to call it "Cow Hollow", and the name has remained, though there have not been meadows or cows there for many a long year. The area began to be developed about a century ago, and there has been a genuine example of urban renewal here in the last 25 years. The numerous Victorian houses (see entry) have been restored, some being converted for commercial purposes.

Now there are fashion boutiques, antique shops, galleries, restaurants, some of the best-known singles bars and cafés. It is an area that has retrieved its style.

Location
1600–2300 Union Street

Bus route
41

61

The side streets off Union Street between Octavia and Steiner Streets are also noteworthy, especially the houses at 2038 and 1980 Union Street, which were built by James-Cudworth, a dairy-farmer, in the 1870s. The house at 2038 is the largest farmhouse remaining here.

Crocker Center

See Galleria at Crocker Center

De Young Memorial Museum

See Golden Gate Park

*Embarcadero Center (Shopping and Leisure Centre)   I8(J/K4)

Location
Between Sacramento, Clay and Battery Streets, and Justin Herman Plaza

Underground station
MUNI Metro
(Embarcadero)

Bus routes
2, 7, 8, 21, 31, 42, 55, 71, 72

The Embarcadero Center complex must be regarded as one of the most interesting and original examples of urban renewal. The $645 million development – incorporating five skyscrapers, two hotels, and a restored office building – are the work of Atlanta architect John Portman. The first four towers and the Hyatt Regency Hotel were constructed between 1968 and 1981. The second phase was completed in 1988 with the addition of a fifth tower, the Park Hyatt Hotel, and the restoration of the Federal Reserve Bank building. Pedestrianised walkways above street level connect the buildings, providing access to 175 shops and restaurants, and also to the adjoining Golden Gateway Center.
As the weather is so mild, people here tend to spend a lot of time in the open air. The plazas between the buildings are on different levels; in several places sculptures by various artists have been set up, and particularly at midday the seats which are provided in large numbers, tempt you to linger for a while.

Hyatt Regency Hotel

Although the architecture of the skyscrapers is conventional, the Hyatt Regency Hotel has not ceased to provoke comment since it was opened in 1973. The ground-plan is virtually a triangle, and the building leans out to the N at an angle of 45 degrees. From the rooms there is a view out over the Bay.
Even more sensational is the hotel's foyer. It is over 300 ft (91 m) long and 190 ft (57 m) high, reaching up to the 17th storey. The restaurant, bars and shops are grouped round it. The centre piece of this unique hall is a four-storey-high ball made of gilded aluminium piping, a work by the sculptor Charles Perry.

Ferry Building   J8(K4)

Location
Foot of Market Street

At the foot of Market Street (see entry) stands, E of Embarcadero Plaza, Ferry Building with its Neo-Romanesque façade and its 230 ft (70 m) high tower, modelled on the Giralda, the campanile of Seville Cathedral. The building

The vast foyer of the Hyatt Regency Hotel with its immense sculptured ball

and its tower were built by the State of California between 1896 and 1903. They survived the 1906 earthquake intact. Once Ferry Building was the real symbol of San Francisco, but it has subsequently been overtaken by others, notably by the Transamerica Pyramid (see entry). Until the building of the San Francisco–Oakland Bridge and the Golden Gate Bridge (see entries) the area around Ferry Building was the spot where all roads met. Every day 170 ferries belonging to various lines kept up a shuttle service to the other side of the bay. Now there are just a few boats serving Oakland, Sausalito and Tiburon (see entries) and Alameda, Larkspur and Vallejo.

The building now houses both the Port Authority and the World Trade Center.

The World Trade Center occupies the N wing. It has an exhibition of products from all parts of the globe. The World Trade Center is open from Monday to Friday from 9 a.m. to 3 p.m. Entry is free.

World Trade Center

*Fisherman's Wharf   H7

Fisherman's Wharf used to be a flourishing fishing harbour and a genuine "Little Italy", for towards the end of the 19th c. Genoese came and settled here, to be followed by Neapolitans, Calabrians and Sicilians. Their influence is sensed there even now.

Location
Jefferson Street

Bus routes
30, 32, 42

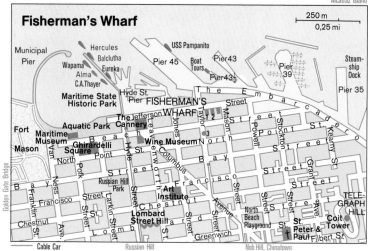

Fisherman's Wharf

Alcatraz Island

250 m
0,25 mi

Municipal
Pier

Hercules
Balclutha
Wapama
Alma
Eureka
C.A.Thayer

USS Pampanito
Pier 45
Boat Tours
Pier 43
Pier 43½
Pier 39

Steamship Dock

Pier 35

Maritime State
Historic Park

Hyde St.
Pier

FISHERMAN'S
WHARF

The
Embarcadero

The
Jefferson

Street

Fort
Mason

Aquatic Park
Maritime
Museum
Ghirardelli
Square

Cannery

Wine Museum

North

Beach

Bay

3

Jones
Taylor
Mason
Powell
Stockton
St. Kearny St.

Street

Street

Russian Hill
Park

Art
Institute

Francisco

Lombard
Street Hill

Chestn

Greenwich

Columbus

North
Beach
Playground

Avenue

St. Peter &
Paul

Coit
Tower

TELE-GRAPH
HILL

Filbert St.

Fort
Maritime
Museum
Mason

North
Point
Beach
Van
Ness
Polk
Larkin
Hyde
Leavenworth

Bay
Franklin
Francisco
Street
Street

Chestnut
Ave.
St.
Street
St.
Lombard

Golden Gate Bridge

Cable Car

Russian Hill

Nob Hill, Chinatown

1 Ripley's "Believe it or Not" Museum   2 Wax Museum   3 St. Francis Statue

View of the harbour for small craft at Fisherman's Wharf

Though the harbour has become rather run down, with many shops, restaurants, a waxworks and other similar attractions, there are few of the 12 million tourists coming to San Francisco each year who do not find time to go to Fisherman's Wharf. And there are still some fishermen who will take tourists out with them for a fee; their boats lie near the block between Jones Street and Leavenworth Street, N of Jefferson Street. Their usual daily catches include crayfish and crabs, soles, salmon, etc. Most of the fish is delivered to restaurants.

Plans are under consideration to give back to the fishermen some at least of what they have lost in recent decades to enterprises aimed mainly at the tourist trade. This would restore to the area something of its original local colour.

Cable Cars
59, 60 (to terminus)

The little museums on Fisherman's Wharf are amusing and worth a visit.

Museums

The "Believe It or Not" Museum (175 Jefferson Street) has some 2000 curiosities from all corners of the globe. It is open every day from 10 a.m. until 10 p.m. (midnight Fri. and Sat.).

Ripley's Museum

To the E, at 145 Jefferson Street, is the Wax Museum at Fisherman's Wharf where 270 life-size wax figures of prominent people are on show in 70 dramatic settings, with its own Chamber of Horrors. Part of the wax museum complex is the Medieval Dungeon in which 14th-century life is electronically recreated. Two further attractions are the

Wax Museum

Fort Point – never called on for heroism in the defence of San Francisco

Haunted Gold Mine and Lazer Maze. The complex is open 9 a.m. to 11.30 p.m. (to midnight Fri. and Sat.).

Fort Point National Historic Site   D7

Location
Golden Gate National
Recreation Area

Bus routes
Golden Gate Transit (from
Market Street and 7th
Street) or No. 30 to
Chestnut and Fillmore and
change to No. 28 to Toll
Plaza

Opening times
Daily 10 a.m.–5 p.m.

Closed
New Year's Day,
Thanksgiving and
Christmas Day

Fort Point lies below Golden Gate Bridge (see entry) and is just a few minutes' walk from Toll Plaza. It was built between 1853 and 1861 to protect San Francisco from attack. But the 600 soldiers stationed here never fired a shot in anger, and the 120 cannon were used only for ceremonial salutes. The fort was evacuated in 1896. It was used as a sort of construction base between 1933 and 1937 while the Golden Gate Bridge was being built. A garrison of about 100 soldiers was stationed here during the Second World War.

In 1970 it was declared a National Historic Site by the US Congress, and since then it has been gradually restored. It is well worth a visit, especially if you go on one of the free daily guided tours, for it is one of the earliest military buildings in the American West. In the last century it was said to be the largest brick structure W of the Mississippi. Entry is free.

Galleria at Crocker Center   I9

Entrances
Post and Sutter Streets

On the corner of Post and Kearny Streets rises the 38-storey skyscraper of the Crocker Bank, built in 1983. It has a façade of pink granite and was designed by the firm of architects Skidmore, Owings & Merrill. All in all it is one of the most attractive of modern buildings; the bank premises include the impressive Galleria, an arcade of elegant shops where daylight floods in. It is reminiscent of the Galleria Vittorio Emmanuelle in Milan.

More than 50 shops and restaurants are open during the usual hours from Monday to Saturday. The two roof gardens, where you can consume your own food, are a veritable oasis in the middle of a busy town.

George R. Moscone Convention Center   I9

Location
South of Market Street,
between Howard Street
and Folsom Street
Entrance: 747 Howard
Street

This convention centre for congresses and exhibitions, opened in December 1981, lies to the S of Market Street on a site of barely 11.5 acres (4·5 ha.), bounded by the 3rd, Howard, 4th and Folsom Streets. It consists of an exhibition hall covering 650,000 sq. ft (60,385 sq. m), the largest column-free indoor space in the USA, 41 conference rooms, seating from 30 to 7000 and a ballroom. The completionn of an expansion programme in 1992 will nearly double the Center's present capacity. Adjoining the centre are the Buena Yerba Gardens which are to become a cultural, recreational and business complex. Guided tours – every Saturday at 1 p.m. from the Moscone Center entrance in Howard Street (information, tel. 558–3770).

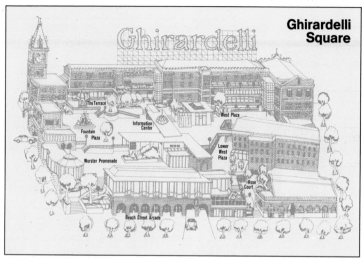

Impression of Ghirardelli Square

*Ghirardelli Square (Shopping and Leisure Centre)

H7

Ghirardelli Square was inaugurated in 1964. It was the first of a number of projects designed to give a new life to abandoned factory complexes (others are The Cannery, Pier 39 and The Anchorage – see entries.) Ghirardelli's old chocolate factory, a red-brick building, has been turned into a centre for shoppers, art-lovers and those in search of entertainment or a good meal. It has gardens with fountains and terraces with fine views.

Domingo Ghirardelli hailed from the Italian city of Rapallo and came by way of Uruguay and Peru to the newly founded city of San Francisco in 1849, the first year of the Gold Rush. He traded in spices, coffee and cocoa and then began chocolate-making. His sons purchased the site where Ghirardelli Square now is together with the woollen mill that already stood there and built the chocolate factory between 1900 and 1916. In the early 1960s it was standing empty because production had been transferred else-where.

A group of San Francisco businessmen purchased the complex and employed several different architects to create on three levels more than 70 shops, galleries, cafés and a cinema, all of which are well patronised. In particular Ghirardelli Square has become a popular rendezvous for the people of San Francisco on warm evenings, and more and more tourists are visiting the complex. One of the most recent attractions is the opening of an offshoot of Maxwell's Plum, the smart New York restaurant, under the same name. (It is essential to book tables in advance – tel. 441–4140.)

Location
Bounded by North Point, Polk, Beach and Larkin Streets

Bus routes
19, 30

Cable car
60

Ancient and modern – Fort Point and Golden Gate Bridge

The belfry was built in 1916 and housed the main offices of the chocolate factory. It was designed by the architect William Mooser sen. who took the Château of Blois in France as his model.

In Rose Court there is a concrete fountain by Lawrence Halpin, the garden-designer of Ghirardelli Square, and in East Plaza Ruth Asawa's concrete fountain is particularly noteworthy. It portrays two mermaids surrounded by turtles, water-lilies and dancing frogs.

**Golden Gate Bridge   D6/7

Bus routes
Golden Gate Transit (from Transbay Terminal, or Market Street and 7th Street) or No. 30 to Chestnut and Laguna, change at Laguna and take No. 28 to Toll Plaza

Bridge Toll
For vehicles going south. $2. No charge for pedestrians

The Golden Gate Suspension Bridge is nearly 2 miles (3 km) long and it connects San Francisco with Marin County and the other districts further N. It was recently designated by the US Travel Service the greatest man-made sight in the United States. For years it was the symbol of San Francisco, though this distinction is now claimed by the Transamerica Pyramid. The splendid scenery all around makes it the most beautiful bridge in the world.

The bridge was inaugurated on 28 May 1937. It had taken four years to build, and the director of the project was Joseph B. Strauss. Construction proved to be particularly difficult on account of the strong cross-currents and a number of fatal accidents occurred. At the date of its completion it was the longest suspension bridge in the world. On an average day it is used by more than 100,000 cars and trucks.

The bridge, which is illuminated in the evening, is approximately 2 miles (3 km) long and 90 ft (27 m) wide; it stands 220 ft (67 m) above mean sea-level. The supporting towers are 740 ft (225 m) high.

Every week 25 painters use about 2 tons of red lead ("International Orange") to keep the paintwork in good condition. The striking colouring is one more reason why the Golden Gate Bridge is known all round the world.

There are in fact many places from which there are good views of the bridge, and Coit Tower on Telegraph Hill is perhaps the best. But visitors should also gain an impression of this marvellous piece of engineering from close inspection. Before crossing the bridge on foot it is worth recalling that, even when the sun is shining brightly, breezes are almost always blowing in from the Pacific. So warm clothing is needed, and it will also be some protection if mist suddenly comes in. There is a wire-netting screen intended to protect potential suicides – there have already been 600 – who contemplate leaping over into the water.

At the end of the bridge stands a monument to its builder, Joseph B. Strauss. He constructed more than 400 major steel bridges all over the world, including one in Leningrad. For good walkers there is the possibility of going on foot all the way from Hyde Street (terminus of cable car 60) via Golden Gate Promenade to the bridge itself. That is a distance of more than 3 miles (5 km), but is an interesting stroll.

On 24 May 1987, the 50th anniversary of the opening, the Golden Gate Bridge was closed to motor vehicles and open only to pedestrians and cyclists. It is estimated that 250,000 people took advantage of the occasion to assemble on the bridge; in the evening the whole length of the structure was illuminated for the first time.

Jubilee of the Bridge 1987

Golden Gate National Recreation Area (Leisure Park)   D7–A14

In 1972 the US Congress decreed the creation of a large leisure park in San Francisco and Marin County, on the other side of the bay. Part of the intention was to prevent the coastal area from being used for industrial purposes or being built up.

This area was given the name Golden Gate National Recreation Area. Many thousands of the inhabitants of San Francisco come there every weekend. It covers an area of some 615 sq. miles (1593 sq. km). There are islands, shores, harbours for small boats, buildings of historic interest and, in the Marin County region, wildlife reserves, picnic facilities and more than 90 miles (145 km) of footpaths. Maps and booklets are available in Fort Mason.

Address
Offices: Fort Mason, Entry Bay and Franklin Street

Bus routes
30 (to Chestnut and Laguna)

**Golden Gate Park   B–E10

Golden Gate Park is 3 miles (5 km) long and ½ mile (800 m) wide, occupying an area of 1017 acres (4·1 sq. km). It is San Francisco's "lungs", for in the city itself there are only small parks.

Before development began in 1871 there were just arid

Location
Bordered by Fulton Street, Stanyan Street, Lincoln Boulevard and the Great Highway

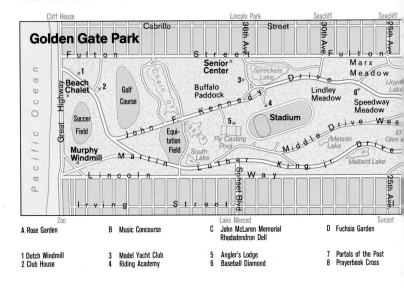

A Rose Garden   B Music Concourse   C John McLaren Memorial Rhododendron Dell   D Fuchsia Garden

1 Dutch Windmill	3 Model Yacht Club
2 Club House	4 Riding Academy

5 Angler's Lodge   7 Portals of the Past
6 Baseball Diamond   8 Prayerbook Cross

Bus routes
5 and 21 (N side, museums),
7 (E side, greenhouses),
71 and 72 (S side, Strybing Arboretum)

Tours
Free guided walking tours of the park at weekends from May to October (tel. 221–1311).

dunes here, and it was only with great difficulty that what was then the largest man-made park in the world was given its present appearance. It was above all the work of Park Commissioner John McLaren who was responsible for the park between 1887 and 1943.

Nowadays there is a grand network of footpaths and cycle tracks for the visitors to enjoy, more than 6000 different kinds of plants and dozens of species of trees, several lakes, bridle-paths, a reserve with buffaloes, three museums, a Japanese tea-garden, greenhouses, a botanical garden and much else besides. Strolling through Golden Gate Park is a delight, but it takes up a lot of time. It should also be recalled that it often becomes unpleasant to stay there after 3 p.m. when mist comes rolling in from the Pacific. The sketch-plan of the park shows the general layout.

*California Academy of Sciences (Museum)

Location
Golden Gate Park

Bus route
5

Opening times
Daily 10 a.m.–5 p.m. (open later in summer)

The California Academy of Sciences stands in the E end of Golden Gate Park. It is the most important scientific institution in the State. Created in 1853, only four years after the foundation of San Francisco, it attracts a million and a half visitors every year.

The collections are mainly devoted to natural history. "Life Through Time" explores the 3·5 billion year history of life on Earth; "Wattis Hall of Human Cultures" has life-size

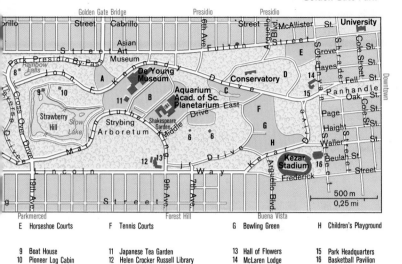

E Horseshoe Courts F Tennis Courts G Bowling Green H Children's Playground

| 9 Boat House | 11 Japanese Tea Garden | 13 Hall of Flowers | 15 Park Headquarters |
| 10 Pioneer Log Cabin | 12 Helen Crocker Russell Library | 14 McLaren Lodge | 16 Basketball Pavilion |

displays illustrating the evolution of Man; "Earth and Space" explores Earth and space phenomena, there is an earthquake simulator and gems and minerals from around the world; while "Wild California" illustrates the wildlife of the Golden State.

Entrance fee charged
(Free 1st Wed. of each month.) Additional charge for the Planetarium and Laserium at all times.

The Steinhart Aquarium at the end of the court with the great fountain has a collection of more than 14,000 aquatic creatures and is one of the biggest of its type in the world. In its 250 tanks, 10,000 fish, dolphins, reptiles (e.g. alligators), etc. are on show. Its "Fish Roundabout" "puts" visitors in the middle of fish in the open ocean.

Steinhart Aquarium

The Morrison Planetarium houses the first "Theater of the Stars" that was not imported from Germany but constructed in the United States in 1951–2. 3800 star patterns are projected on to a dome 65 ft (20 m) in diameter. One-hour sky shows are presented daily, tel. 750–7141 for schedule.

Morrison Planetarium

An unusual attraction is the Laserium where concerts with laser lights are presented on select evenings, tel. 750–7138 for schedule.

Laserium

*M. H. de Young Memorial Museum

The M. H. de Young Memorial Museum is the oldest museum in San Francisco.
The building was erected in 1894 as an art gallery when an

Bus route
5 (to Fulton Street and 8th Avenue)

M.H.de Young Memorial Museum

Asian Art Museum

(Avery Brundage Collection)

A Cloakroom   B Telephone   C Bookstall   D Café   00 Toilets

Rooms 1 & 2	Old World	Room 20	17th c. (Great Britain)
Room 3	Medieval and Renaissance (Spanish)	Room 21	British Art
Room 4	El Greco	Rooms 22 & 25	Temporary Exhibitions
Room 5	Renaissance of the North		
Room 6	17th c. (North Italy)	Room 23	18th c. (France)
Rooms 7, 9, 10, 11	Renaissance (Italy)	Rooms 33 & 34	Oakes Galleries; 17th and 18th c. (Italy)
Room 8	18th c. (Germany)	Room 35	19th c. (Europe)
Rooms 12, 13, 15	Kress Galleries (Period of Rembrandt)	Rooms 36 to 38	Temporary Exhibitions
Rooms 14 & 16	Kress Galleries (Rubens, Van Dyck and contemporaries)	Rooms 39 to 48	American Galleries
Room 17	Gainsborough, Reynolds and other British artists)	Room 49	Africa, Oceania and America
Room 18	18th c. (England)		Rooms not mentioned (e.g. 24, 26 to 32) are at present closed.
Room 19	18th and 19th c. (Great Britain)		

Opening times
Wed.–Sun. 10 a.m.–5 p.m.

Entrance fee charged
1st Wed. of month (all day)
and 1st Sat. 10 a.m. and
noon entrance free

International Californian Exposition was held in Golden Gate Park. It was later handed over to the general director of the exhibition, the newspaper owner Michael H. de Young (1849–1925) who was entrusted with setting up a permanent museum there. The original stock consisted of a few works which had been shown at the exhibition. Gifts made possible the continuous, planned build up of the collection. Consequently, in the course of the next quarter of a century, further extensions were needed until at last in 1921 the original building in Egyptian style, as is shown now only by two sphinxes which remain here, had to be replaced by modern museum premises.

It was at this point in time that the museum also received its present name, to commemorate its founder and benefactor. At present it has some 40 galleries and more than 200,000 sq. ft (18,500 sq. m) of exhibition space. Art from all over the world is on display.

Examples of the M. H. de Young Memorial Museum collections – art from Papua New Guinea . . .

. . . the art of the North American Indians

. . . and the art of the North American Eskimo

The museum's collection accordingly includes examples from Egypt, Greece and Rome, from the Middle Ages and the Renaissance. Folk art from Africa, the South Seas and America is represented by first-rate pieces.

Unlike most American museums, this one is not under private management but receives all its support from the city which, a few years ago, found itself obliged to charge for admission. The ticket does, however, also cover a same-day visit to the adjoining Asian Art Museum of San Francisco (see below) and the Californian Palace of the Legion of Honor (see entry).

Opening hours have also been reduced. The museum used to be open seven days a week, but now it is closed on Mondays and Tuesdays.

North American Art

Especially noteworthy is the collection (21 galleries in all) of paintings, sculptures and furnishings from North America from the mid-17th to the mid-20th c., especially since the gift to the museum by John D. Rockefeller of a comprehensive collection of American art, containing, among other exhibits, 175 paintings.

Here is displayed the oldest work of art in the museum and probably the oldest picture to have been painted in North America: it is the work of an anonymous Massachusetts artist and dates from about 1670.

Primitive Art

Room 49 which is adjacent to the American Galleries houses an exhibition of so-called primitive art. The exhibits are splendidly displayed, and this is, in fact, the only room which has been fully modernised.

One of the most important collections is made of works of art from Europe. Apart from a few on special display in rooms temporarily available, these may be seen in Galleries 3–23 and 33–5. Most of these galleries stand round an inner courtyard which bears the name of the newspaper-owner William Hearst.

Hearst (the owner of the "San Francisco Examiner") did not want to do less for the museum than his colleague M. H. de Young (owner of the "San Francisco Chronicle").

Among the finest works here are three paintings by El Greco ("John the Baptist", "St Peter" and "Saint Francis"), a canvas by Rubens and a marble sculpture by Benvenuto Cellini.

Parts of Samuel H. Kress's Collection are to be seen in Galleries 12, 13 and 15. There are works by Spanish, Dutch and Italian painters from the 14th to the 18th c., among them Fra Angelico, Titian, Pieter de Hooch and Goya.

In the Roscoe and Margaret Oakes Collection in Galleries 36 and 37 Dutch, Flemish and English art of the 17th to 19th c. is represented with works by Rembrandt, Frans Hals, Van Dyck, Gainsborough, Reynolds and Raeburn.

European Art

Especially noteworthy are a few rooms which have been completely fitted out in period style. Some of them were brought over from European houses and set up here as authentically as possible.

Gallery 4 has, for instance, a Mudejar-style carved wooden ceiling from Toledo. In Gallery 8 there is a splendid room from a patrician house in Aachen which dates from the 18th c., and Gallery 20 has been fitted out in English Elizabethan style.

Interiors

American painting of the 18th and 19th c. is represented by John Singleton Copley, Charles Willson Peale, Benjamin West, John Trumbull, Thomas Cole, George Caleb Bingham, and others.

American Painters

*Asian Art Museum of San Francisco

The Asian Art Museum of San Francisco, opened in 1966 and occupying the W wing of the M. H. de Young Memorial Museum, is one of the most unusual museums in America. What makes it unusual – and in this it is comparable only with the Hirshhorn Museum in New York – is that its exhibits are 95% the collection of one man, Avery Brundage, the rich businessman who was famous as president for so many years of the International Olympic Committee.

Brundage began to take an interest in the art of the Far East in 1936. He built up a private collection which, in 1959, he offered to the city of San Francisco "to bridge the gap between East and West". The people of San Francisco decided to build a special museum; it was not finished until 1966 and from the outside it is undistinguished.

During the intervening period of seven years Brundage had continued to build up his collection, and he presented the additional works to San Francisco as well. Finally the museum received after his death, which occurred in 1975 when he was 88, the legacy of the rest of his collection of

Bus route
5 (to Fulton Street and 8th Avenue)

Opening times
Wed.–Sun. 10 a.m.–5 p.m. (1st Wed. of month until 8.45 p.m.)

Closed
Mon. and Tues.

Entrance fee charged
Free 1st Wed. (all day) and 1st Sat. (10 a.m.–noon) of month.
Other times fee includes same-day entrance to M. H. de Young Memorial and California Palace of the Legion of Honor Museums.

From the collections of the Asian Art Museum – sculptures from Khmer culture . . .

. . . and Japanese 12th c. guardian figurines

works of art. As a consequence there are now here nearly 10,000 sculptures, paintings, bronzes, ceramic objects and jade-carvings, and architectural pieces from Japan, Korea, China, India, Iran and other Asiatic cultures.

It is hoped that it will be possible to develop the museum in the course of the years into a major centre for Asiatic art and culture in the Western World. Its present collections and publications justify these hopes. It is one of the most important museums in San Francisco and has something to offer every visitor, not just specialists in Asiatic art.

Almost half the Brundage collection consists of examples of Chinese origin. They occupy the ground floor, there is a Jade Room well worth seeing for its own sake, and sharing the ground floor is the recently expanded Korea Gallery. On the upper floor are works of art from other lands – Iran, Turkey, Syria, Afghanistan, India, Pakistan, Mongolia, Japan and Indonesia.

Development

As there are frequently also special exhibitions of Asiatic art loaned by private collectors or other museums, barely 10% of the whole collection can be displayed. To overcome this difficulty, the exhibits are changed from time to time. It is because this principle of rotation is observed that no individual examples can be picked out and described here.

Sketch plans make it possible to find one's way round the galleries. The objects on show are all placed in chronological order.

The examples of Chinese lacquerwork and ebony carving are exceptional, but on the other hand Brundage collected only a few Chinese paintings. This left some gaps to be filled, and it was possible to do so thanks to the generous purchase fund. The museum now has more than 150 Chinese rolls and bark paintings, though only a few of these are at present on show.

Chinese Department

The chief attraction of the museum is the Jade Room. With about 1200 works of art in jade it is the largest in any Western land. It covers virtually all the Chinese periods, beginning with the 5th c. B.C., but the stress is mainly on the Ming and Ch'ing periods (about A.D. 1400–1900).

Jade Room

Though relatively small, the Japanese Department contains choice pieces from almost every period.

Japanese Department

As Brundage became interested in collecting the art of India, Indonesia and Indochina only in his later years, these departments are inferior to the collections of Chinese art in both quantity and quality.

There is a library with 12,000 volumes on art in the Near and Far East open to visitors and specialists. Students and museum staff from the USA, Japan, Taiwan and Korea are given specialist training in Asiatic art.

Library

The museum has a branch in Japantown (see entry).

*Japanese Tea-Garden (Zen-Garden)

A further attraction of Golden Gate Park and one of the real sights of the city is the Japanese Tea-Garden. Like the M. H. de Young Memorial Museum it dates back to the 1894 California International Exposition. At the time it was the

Opening times
9 a.m.–6.30 p.m. Mar.–Sept.; 8.30 a.m.–5.30 p.m. Oct.–Feb.

Impression of the Japanese Tea-Garden in Golden Gate Park

Bird's-eye view of the Conservatory of Flowers

setting for a Japanese village and one of the elements in it. Now it may be considered a further element of the Asian Art Museum next to which it is situated.

The layout of the garden was entrusted to Makoto Hagiwara, a Japanese, and he looked after it for the next three decades and lived on the site. The work was then continued between 1925 and 1942 by his daughter, his son-in-law and his grandson. Like many other Japanese, the Hagiwaras were then interned, the Japanese Tea-Garden becoming an Oriental Tea-Garden and several of the houses there were destroyed. One dwelling was converted into a souvenir shop. It was only in 1952 that the garden was given back its original name. The next year a lantern of peace was hung up and the Zen-Garden was laid out; these gifts were from the children of Japan to the American people. Since then its Japanese-Buddhist character has been stressed more and more strongly. The gaily coloured pagoda and the moon bridge are especial attractions. The garden is a particularly lovely sight in spring when the many cherry trees are in bloom and the cherry blossom festival is celebrated in Japantown (see entry).

Entrance fee charged
(Free 1st Wed. of month)

Strybing Arboretum (Botanical Garden)

Beside the road opposite the Japanese Tea-Garden lies the Strybing Arboretum. It occupies some 62 acres within Golden Gate Park. It was named for Helen Strybing who endowed it. There are more than 6000 species of plant to be seen here. They are grouped according to their region of origin and clearly labelled. The ducks and swans may be fed by visitors, and peacocks with their decorative tails add colour to the green of the lawns and the gravelled paths. At the entrance a plan may be obtained which is useful for getting a general idea of the layout. It is a good idea to take a guided tour; it takes in all the beauties of this special attraction of Golden Gate Park.

Bus route
71, 72 (to 9th Avenue and Lincoln Way)

Opening times
Mon.–Fri. 8 a.m.–4.30 p.m.; Sat., Sun. and public holidays 10 a.m.–5 p.m.

Tours
Daily 1.30 p.m. (also 10.30 a.m. Sat. and Sun.) Meeting point: Kiosk

Entry free

Conservatory of Flowers (Plant House)

The Conservatory of Flowers is the oldest building in Golden Gate Park and probably the best example of Victorian architecture in or around San Francisco. It was purchased in England, transported by ship round Cape Horn to San Francisco and was re-erected here in 1879. It is now a protected building. In the conservatory may be seen, as well as a tropical garden, orchids, ferns and other foliage plants, displays of various varieties of flowers – arum lilies, begonias, chrysanthemums and many others – according to the season.

Bus route
5 or 21 to Arguello and Fulton, then walk into Park (about 500 ft/150 m)

Opening times
Daily, 9 a.m.–6 p.m. Apr.–Oct. (until 5 p.m. Nov.–Mar.)

Entrance fee charged

Grace Cathedral   H8(I4)

This Neo-Gothic church, obviously influenced by the architecture of Notre Dame in Paris, was dedicated in 1964, after it had taken 36 years to build. The earlier church, which stood lower down on the slope of Nob Hill, was destroyed in the earthquake of 1906. Grace Cathedral is the seat of the Episcopalian Bishop of California.

Situation
1051 Taylor Street

Cable car
61 (California Street)

Grace Cathedral on Nob Hill – it took 36 years to build and was completed in 1964

Opening times
Daily 7.30 a.m.–6 p.m. (to 6.30 p.m. Thurs.)

Tours
Tues.–Sun. 1 p.m.–3 p.m.; Mon. 10 a.m.–noon

Entry free

Although Notre Dame was the architectural model for the building as a whole, Florentine works of art were the inspiration of the main portals which take the form of casts from Lorenzo Ghiberti's "Gates of Paradise" at the Baptistery in Florence.

The interior houses a number of notable works of art, including a 13th c. Catalonian Crucifix, a Flemish altarpiece of the late 15th c., a silk and gold Brussels Gobelin tapestry dating from the 16th c., a terracotta relief of the Madonna and Child by the Renaissance artist Antonio Rossellino and, on the N wall of the ambulatory, a collection of pages from medieval Bibles illustrating the history of Bible reproduction. Of particular interest are stained-glass windows from the workshops of Charles Connick, Henry Lee Willet, Mark Adams and Gabriel Loire. The great east rose-window (by G. Loire, 1963) is illuminated after dark from within the building. The Cathedral has a celebrated choir of men and boys; recitals are often given on the organ which has 7286 pipes.

The 44 bells in the N tower can be heard every evening; the hour bell, weighing six tonnes, is the largest in the West.

Haas-Lilienthal House   G8(G/H4)

Address
2007 Franklin Street

Bus route
2

Haas-Lilienthal House is one of the largest private residences in San Francisco. It has remained quite unspoilt for nearly a century, with just a few additions built on. It was constructed in 1886 to the plans of the architect Peter R. Schmidt for William Haas, a wholesale grocer who had immigrated from Bavaria. The so-called Eastlake style

Haas-Lilienthal House – a private residence in the Eastlake style

was chosen, with a Queen Anne tower. The asymmetrical placing of cubes, cones, pyramids, cylinders and other geometrical forms is the most striking feature.

Inside it had something which was unusual at the date when the house was built; it was fully wired for electricity, though, for safety's sake, candle sconces were provided in the candelabra. Taking everything into account, the builder's bill at the time is supposed to have amounted to only $18,500.

Until about ten years ago the house was still lived in by descendants of its original owner. Since then it has been taken over as the offices of the Foundation for San Francisco's Architectural Heritage which works to maintain all that is important in the city's architecture.

The Ball Room is still used for its original purpose: it is hired out for various social functions.

Opening times
Wed. noon–4 p.m.;
Sun. 11 a.m.–4.30 p.m.

Entrance fee charged
Includes tour

Hyde Street Pier

See National Maritime Museum

Jackson Square   I8(J/K4)

Jackson Square is one of the most interesting parts of San Francisco from an historical point of view. But, contrary to what might be expected, it is not a square. It comprises Block 400 on Jackson Street and a few side streets where a number of 19th c. business premises remain.

Situation
Bordered by Pacific Street,
Montgomery Street,
Washington Street and
Battery Street

These are now used primarily as show rooms by interior designers. But there are also several other shops which repay a visit.

In 1972 Jackson Square was the first part of San Francisco to be declared an area of historical interest, and most of the houses are now listed as protected buildings. Among them are:

No. 407: the warehouse of the Ghirardelli Chocolate Factory; built in 1860 and in use until 1894.

Nos. 415–31: the Ghirardelli Chocolate Factory; built in 1853 and in use until 1894.

No. 432: here Tremont Hotel used to stand. It was built in 1855, and when it was demolished elements from it were incorporated in the present house.

No. 441: the building was erected in 1861 on top of the buried wrecks of two ships abandoned during the Gold Rush.

No. 470: this building which dates from 1852 housed in succession the consulates of Spain, Chile and France and was also the editorial office of "La Parola", an Italian language newspaper.

No. 472: one of the oldest and, in its simplicity, most handsome office buildings in San Francisco of the years 1850–2; between 1865 and 1875 it housed the French Consulate.

Nos. 445, 463–73 and 451. The first two date from 1860, the latter from 1866. They were built by Anson Parsons Hotaling, an important liquor-dealer of the period.

Most of these buildings survived the 1906 earthquake, though a few were slightly damaged and were later repaired.

Round the corner is 722–28 Montgomery Street, a former tobacco warehouse. Melvin Belli, the famous defence attorney and specialist in damages actions, had it converted into his law offices in 1958.

Japanese Tea-Garden

See Golden Gate Park

Japantown (District of the City)   G9

Situation
Bordered by Post Street,
Geary Street, Laguna
Street and Fillmore Street

Bus routes
2, 3, 4 and 38 (to Laguna
Street)

The Japantown district of San Francisco is the cultural and business centre for the Japanese citizens of the city. The first Japanese to come to San Francisco arrived more than 120 years ago. They called the city Soko. It was, however, only after the 1906 earthquake that they started to settle in what is now called Japantown. In Japanese the district is called Nihonmachi. During the Second World War most of the Japanese and Japanese-Americans ("Nisei") were forcibly interned. On being set free many of the former returned to their distant homeland.

Japantown: Peace Plaza with its five-storey Peace Pagoda

It was only slowly that the others returned to the district in which they had formerly resided. Today, however, the Japanese population of San Francisco amounts to more than 12,000.

The opening of the Japan Center in 1968 gave the district a great stimulus. Now there are Japanese hotels here, many Japanese and Korean restaurants, sushi bars, shops, art galleries, theatres, and Japanese baths.

The great sight of the district is the Japanese Peace Pagoda, but the temple and the shrines, the art exhibitions and the numerous shops are also well worth a visit.

In spring there is a cherry blossom festival (Sakura Matsuri; see Practical Information – Events) on Peace Plaza with its five-storey Peace Pagoda. Entry is through a gate ("romon") designed by Yoshiro Taniguchi.

Justin Herman Plaza

I8(K4)

This small park was created in the course of the development of the Embarcadero Center (see entry). It lies just in front of the Hyatt Regency Hotel. Office workers from the down-town skyscrapers like to come here during their mid-day break to eat their lunches on the benches. Musicians and street actors come and perform at this time, too. The Vaillancourt Fountain is especially remarkable. It was constructed by the Canadian sculptor Armand Vaillancourt out of colossal concrete blocks on which the public is allowed to climb.

Situation
Where Market Street begins, opposite the Ferry Building

83

Justin Herman Plaza

*Lombard Street   H7(H3)

Situation
Hyde Street to
Leavenworth Street

Cable car
60 (to the corner of Hyde
Street and Lombard Street)

A short section of this street on Russian Hill has become one of the greatest sights of the city. It is called the "crookedest street" in the world. Stretching the length of just a single block, it has a fall of one in two and a half and ten Z bends.

Few tourists with cars miss the opportunity of seeing this. Generally they drive up Lombard Street from the shore side and from the summit at the corner of Hyde Street they come back down to Columbus Avenue. For pedestrians it is easier and less dangerous as they can use stone steps.

The "crooked" section of Lombard Street is planted out with hydrangeas which give it a delightful appearance.

Louise M. Davies Symphony Hall

See Civic Center

Maiden Lane   I9(I/J5)

Situation
E side of Union Square,
between Post Street and
Geary Street

Maiden Lane was once notorious on account of its pot-houses and brothels, but it has now become one of the smartest shopping streets in San Francisco. Here are found only specialist shops with choice goods.

Lombard Street: the "crookedest street" in the world ▶

View of Market Street and the business district

No. 140 is a house of particular architectural interest. It is the only building in San Francisco by the famous architect Frank Lloyd Wright. In the opinion of many this house with its inner ramp is, so to speak, an early sketch for Wright's design for the Guggenheim Museum in New York. But this frequently expressed opinion is incorrect, even though the house at 140 Maiden Lane was completed in 1953, four years before work commenced on the New York Museum, because Wright had put forward his plans for the museum as early as the late 1940s. The house is at present the Circle Art Gallery.

Main Public Library

See Civic Center

Market Street   I8–F12(K4–H6)

Impressive Market Street, one of the few thoroughfares cutting diagonally across the grid-iron street pattern of San Francisco, forms the boundary between the down-at-heel south of the city and the up-and-coming north.
All this harks back to a city plan prepared in 1847 by the engineer Jasper O'Farrell at the behest of the military authorities. In the N part he planned comparatively narrow streets, while the S part, which was marshland at the time,

was to have wide streets, some 15 ft (5 m) wider than in the N, and individual blocks.

Market Street was designed as a main street almost 130 ft (40 m) wide. As the two street networks did not, however, coincide, travelling N–S via Market Street has remained difficult to the present day. The numbering of the houses in all the streets starts from Market Street, and the streets that traverse it alter their direction. It is a standing joke among the people of San Francisco that "there's hardly another street with so many crossroads and so little hope of getting straight across".

The districts with the broad streets S of Market Street were, however, those that went down and down, and there was a danger that the inhabitants of the slums might swamp the northern districts. It was thought that the only way to reverse the trend was by a thorough redevelopment of Market Street. Accordingly, between 1964 and 1979, more than 50 million dollars was put into revitalising this street which has been quite transformed in appearance, at least from Ferry Building to Powell Street. Trees have been planted in the street, the sidewalks have been repaved with red stone, bus shelters have been erected, and the appearance of street has been changed as a result of the construction of the numerous skyscrapers. But beyond Powell Street the overall plan which is the brainchild of the architect John Carl Warnecke has not yet produced the desired effect.

Market Street goes SW to Twin Peaks, NE to Embarcadero Plaza and to the Ferry Building (see entries) on San Francisco Bay. On the left where Powell Street leads into Market Street is the S turntable for the cable cars. Behind it rise the 46-storey San Francisco Hilton Hotel on Hilton Square which was completed in 1971 with a viewing platform at a height of 475 ft (145 m) and the Parc Fifty Five Hotel, opened in 1984. N behind the cable car turntable stands the Westin St Francis Hotel, built in 1904. It has a 380 ft (116 m) high tower added in 1972 with a panoramic bar at the top. Union Square (see entry) is off to the right.

Mexican Museum   G7

The Mexican Museum is the only museum in the United States devoted entirely to Mexican art and folk culture from the Pre-Columbian period to the present day. It is particularly rich in ceramics. Other interesting exhibits include paintings by Chicanos, that is the Mexican farm-hands who come to the United States to help gather in the harvest.

Every second Saturday of the month, at 10 a.m., the museum organises a guided tour round the many murals in the Mission District quarter of the city where the museum is situated. Many of these murals show the strong influence of Mexican artists such as Rivera and Orozco.

Address
Fort Mason, Building D

Bus route 30

Opening times
Wed.–Sun. noon–5 p.m.
(until 8 p.m. the 1st Wed.
of month)

Closed Public holidays

Entrance fee charged
(Free 1st Wed. of month)

M. H. de Young Memorial Museum

See Golden Gate Park

Statue of Father Junípero Serra, the founder of Mission Dolores

*Mission Dolores   G11

Situation
Dolores Street and 16th
Street

Underground station
MUNI Metro J (to 16th
Street)

Opening times
May–Sept. daily,
9 a.m.–4.30 p.m.; Oct.–Apr.
daily, 9 a.m.–4 p.m.

Closed
Thanksgiving, Christmas
Day, New Year's Day

Entrance fee charged

Mission Dolores, or, to give it its proper title, the Mission
San Francisco de Assisi, is the sixth of the 21 missions
founded by Franciscans from Mexico on the California coast. Father Junípero Serra (born 1713 in Petrá in
Majorca, died 1784 in Monterey – see entry) laid the founda-
tion-stone on 9 October 1776, and the building was completed in 1791. It is thus the oldest building remaining in San
Francisco.

Mission Dolores is 110 ft (34 m) long and 21 ft (6 m) wide
with walls nearly 4 ft (1 m) thick. The roof, which has been
restored, is decorated with pictures painted by Indians in
bright colours. In the mission there were all told 28,000
baptisms, mainly of Indians.

The basilica near the mission building dates from 1918. The
earlier church which stood there was, unlike the mission,
destroyed in the 1906 earthquake. Documents about the
history of the mission are on display in a special room. In
the cemetery, which has subsequently been reduced in
size, burials took place from the 1780s until the end of the
19th c. Among those laid to rest here were more than 5000
Indians who perished in the two great measles epidemics
of 1804 and 1826. Mission Dolores is not simply one of
the few sights S of Market Street (see entry); it is also the
only one of the 27 missions which today stands in the
centre of a great city and which may therefore be visited
easily.

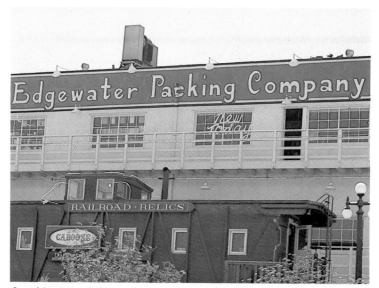

One of the sights of Monterey: a factory in Cannery Row now used for other purposes

*Monterey

Monterey is nowadays a town with some 27,000 inhabitants. It is in a beautiful position on Monterey Bay and has an interesting past. From 1770 to 1822 Monterey was the capital of Spanish California; at that time Los Angeles, San Francisco and Sacramento, the present-day capital, had not yet come into existence. After Mexico had declared its independence from Spain, Monterey remained the provincial capital for another 24 years but soon afterwards began to lose its political importance.

The fish canning industry collapsed years ago as a consequence of the disappearance of the sardine from the waters around Monterey, and in his novel "Cannery Row" John Steinbeck left a literary memorial to it. Now the tourist industry is the chief economic activity. There are many good hotels, motels and restaurants; a complete list is obtainable from the Monterey Peninsula Chamber of Commerce, 380 Alvarado Street, P.O. Box 1770, Monterey, CA 93942, tel. 408–649–1770.

Location
133 miles (214 km) S
(Coastal Highway 1 or
Highway 101)

Two of the most interesting houses – they have both been converted into museums – are the old Custom House, opposite the entry to Fisherman's Wharf, and Stevenson House (530 Houston Street) which was built 150 years ago for a well-to-do family. It is so-called because Scottish writer Robert Louis Stevenson resided here in 1879.
Other houses worth a visit are Pacific House, now a

Houses to visit

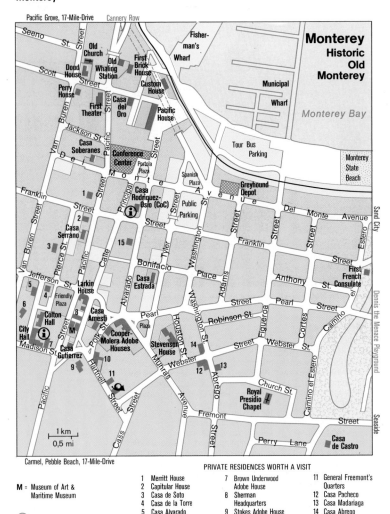

Monterey Historic Old Monterey

Pacific Grove, 17-Mile-Drive   Cannery Row

Seeno St.
Scott Street
Dond House
Perry House
Old Church
Old Whaling Station
First Brick House
First Theater
Casa del Oro
Custom House
Pacific House
Casa Soberanes
Conference Center
Portola Plaza
Spanish Plaza
Franklin Street
Van Buren Street
Pierce Street
Casa Rodriquez-Osio (CoC)
Public Parking
Greyhound Depot
Casa Serrano
Del Monte Avenue
15
Bonifacio
Casa Estrada
Place
Franklin Street
Jefferson St.
Larkin House
Casa Amesti
Adams Street
Anthony St.
First French Consulate
Friendly Plaza
Pearl Plaza
Houston St.
Cooper-Molera Adobe Houses
Stevenson House
Robinson St.
Webster St.
Colton Hall
City Hall
Madison St.
Casa Gutierrez
Munras Avenue
Webster Street
Church St.
Royal Presidio Chapel
Fremont Street
1 km
0,5 mi
Carmel, Pebble Beach, 17-Mile-Drive
Perry Lane
Casa de Castro

Fisher-man's Wharf
Municipal Wharf
Monterey Bay
Tour Bus Parking
Monterey State Beach
Sand City
Dennis the Menace Playground
Camino el Estero
Seaside

M = Museum of Art & Maritime Museum

ⓘ Visitor Information

PRIVATE RESIDENCES WORTH A VISIT

1 Merritt House	7 Brown Underwood	11 General Freemont's
2 Capitular House	Adobe House	Quarters
3 Casa de Soto	8 Sherman	12 Casa Pacheco
4 Casa de la Torre	Headquarters	13 Casa Madariaga
5 Casa Alvarado	9 Stokes Adobe House	14 Casa Abrego
6 Casa Vasquez	10 First Federal Court	15 Casa Sanchez

museum, Larkin House which still contains some period features, and Casa del Oro. Most of these houses belong to Monterey State Historic Park, and they are easily found by visitors who follow the red markings of the "Path of History". Many buildings offer tours year round; days and hours vary (tel. 408–649–1770).

Seal Rock – a landscape feature of "17 Mile Drive"

California's oldest theatre is found here. It was built in 1846 and is still occasionally used for performances.

A visit to Fisherman's Wharf with its shops and reasonably priced fish restaurants is also recommended.

Fisherman's Wharf

The second major attraction of Monterey is Cannery Row. This used to be a street of factories, but a few years ago it was converted into a complex with restaurants, shops, galleries and aquarium (see below). Consequently all that remains of the world described in Steinbeck's novel "Cannery Row" are the walls of the buildings.

Cannery Row

The Monterey Bay Aquarium, opened in 1984, occupies the site of the Hovden Cannery Factory, which was once one of the largest in Cannery Row and which had been in existence from 1916 until 1980 but had not been used since 1972. The architecture of this elaborate complex, the largest of its kind in the USA, was adapted from that of the former factory. The aquarium stands right on the shore of the rocky bay. The emphasis of this splendidly equipped aquarium is on the representation of the exceptionally rich marine life of Monterey Bay. The visitor is offered several ways of observing the coastal formations, marine vegetation, fish and other forms of marine life, as well as coastal and sea birds – through the glass walls of pools, through telescopes, macroscopes, and microscopes as well as by means of underwater video cameras which can be remotely controlled by the observer. Expert guides in diving equipment give commentaries over loudspeakers from the large aquariums, where they can station themselves among the fauna and

**Monterey Bay Aquarium
886 Cannery Row
Opening Times
Daily (except Christmas)
10 a.m.–6 p.m.; 9.30 a.m.–
6 p.m. during summer and
holidays. Daily feeding
shows
Cost of admission is high

flora. In addition it is possible actually to handle several living creatures.

The complex comprises some 80 pools (some of them occupying three storeys) and 20 galleries, both covered in and in the open. Here there live about 6500 creatures of nearly 60 different species (sharks and other large fish, sea-otters, giant octopuses, crustaceans, starfish, etc.).

On the main floor a "Habitat Path" leads the visitor past the diverse sections of the aquarium; the most impressive are known as "Monterey Bay Habitats" (a coastal section 30 yards/27·5 m long), "Kelp Forest" (an enormous tank 28 ft/8·5 m high holding 280,000 gallons/1·26 million litres of water) and the "Great Tide Pool".

In the extensive "Marine Mammals Gallery" are exhibited replicas of mammals which live in the bay, including whales, dolphins, sea-lions and seals. Sea-otters, which are an endangered species, are bred in the aquarium and can be seen romping about in a special pool which extends over two storeys.

There is a restaurant with a sea view and an oyster bar.

17 Mile Drive

Carmel (see entry) lies just a few miles from Monterey, on the S side of the Monterey peninsula. It is well worth taking the rather longer route by way of "17 Mile Drive" (toll) since it offers wonderful views. It leaves the town at Pacific Grove Gate and then continues along the coast, passing for part of the way through Del Monte Wood in which many large villas are situated, and it is impressive because of the large numbers of cypress trees and so-called Monterey pines.

There are colonies of many different types of gull on Seal and Bird Rocks. Sea-lions and seals can often be seen here. From Cypress Lookout there is a particularly fine view N and S out over the Pacific Coast.

Mount Tamalpais   G31

Distance
20 miles (32 km) N

Mount Tamalpais is 2700 ft (823 m) high, the highest point in the immediate vicinity of San Francisco. From the top there is a magnificent view of the Golden Gate. It is possible to drive, by way of the Golden Gate Bridge and US 101, right up to the summit or else cars can be parked at the foot of Tamalpais while visitors use one of the many footpaths.

The area around Mount Tamalpais is now nearly all Californian State Park territory, with large picnic areas and also two fields for campers with tents. As in Muir Woods (see entry) a few miles further on, many Redwood trees *(Sequoia sempervirens)* grow here.

*Muir Woods (Giant Redwood Grove)   G/H31

Location
Mill Valley CA. 15 miles
(24 km) N via US 101 and
Highway 1; Sat. and Sun.
Ferry from Ferry Building
to Larkspur, then bus

Giant Redwood trees grow well only in California and Oregon, and the most famous and tallest specimens in the world grow a few miles from San Francisco in Muir Woods. Since 1908 the Woods have been a National Monument under the protection of the National Park Service which

Muir Woods National Monument: the famous Giant Redwoods grow here . . .

. . . the world's tallest trees

Museum of Modern Art

Opening times
8 a.m.–dusk

Entry free

runs a kiosk at the entrance where visitors can obtain all the information they may need.

Muir Woods are named for the naturalist John Muir who tried to persuade Americans to take an interest in nature conservation back in the 19th c. He founded the Sierra Club in San Francisco which was the first important organisation concerned with ecology.

These woods cover 550 acres (223 ha.), and many of the famous Giant Redwoods grow here. The scientific name is *Sequoia sempervirens*, and their boles are up to 20 ft (6 m) across. They are found growing naturally only in a belt 550 miles (885 km) long and 30 miles (48 km) wide along the Pacific coast from S of Monterey (see entry) up into the SW corner of the State of Oregon. There is heavy rainfall from November to April, and a lot of mist in the mornings and evenings during the dry summer months; these humid conditions are ideal for the growth of these trees.

The tallest Giant Redwoods in Muir Woods reach a height of 252 ft (75 m). In the first hundred years they put on a foot a year, but then the rate of growth diminishes. The oldest Giant Redwood, which has subsequently perished, was 2200 years old. The average age of the trees is between 400 and 800 years. The root network of these trees stretches out sideways as far as 150 ft (46 m), but the roots never go down deeper than 20 ft (6 m).

In Muir Woods there are in all 6 miles (10 km) of footpaths, and they are all well sign-posted. As it is, however, frequently cool and damp here, even in the summer, warm clothing is recommended.

Museum of Modern Art

See Civic Center: San Francisco Museum of Modern Art

Museum of Money of the American West

See Bank of California

*Napa and Sonoma Valleys (Vineyards)

Location
43–53 miles (69–85 km) N by car via the Golden Gate Bridge (US Highway 101) and then on US Highway 121; organised bus tours

Napa Valley and Sonoma Valley are the best-known and the largest vineyards in California. The excellent wines produced are generally gaining a foothold even in the European market. Viticulture was introduced into California about 1825 by Spanish Franciscans and subsequently developed to its present high standard by vintners from Germany, Alsace, France, Hungary and Italy. The wine vaults N of the bay are reckoned moreover to be the best in the United States. Grape harvest goes on from September to the beginning of November. Altogether Napa and Sonoma Valleys have nearly 150 wineries, and the rest of California has a similar number. This is some indication of the importance of this branch of agriculture in California.

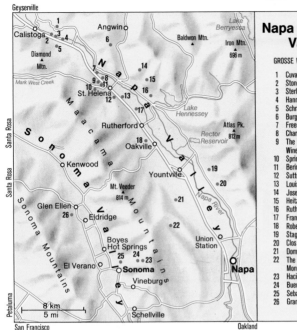

Geyserville

San Francisco   Oakland

Napa & Sonoma Valleys

GROSSE WEINKELLEREIEN

1 Cuvaison
2 Stonegate
3 Sterling Vineyards
4 Hanns Kornell Cellars
5 Schramsberg Vineyards
6 Burgess Cellars
7 Freemark Abbey Winery
8 Charles Krug Winery
9 The Christian Brothers
   Wine & Champagne Cellars
10 Spring Mountain Vineyards
11 Beringer Vineyards
12 Sutter Home Winery
13 Louis M. Martini
14 Joseph Phelps Vineyards
15 Heitz Wine Cellars
16 Rutherford Hill Winery
17 Franciscan Vineyards
18 Robert Mondavi Winery
19 Stag's Leap Wine Cellars
20 Clos du Val
21 Domaine Chandon
22 The Christian Brothers
   Mont La Salle Vineyards
23 Hacienda Wine Cellars
24 Buena Vista Cellars
25 Sebastiani Vineyards
26 Grand Cru Vineyards

In Sonoma Valley some of the largest wineries are near the town of Sonoma itself. Visitors who wish to visit the vaults are welcome.

Sonoma Valley

The Buena Vista Vaults on the E outskirts of Sonoma were founded in 1857 by a Hungarian Count, Agoston Haraszthy. They belong now to Hubertus von Wulffen, a German, and excellent concerts take place here during the summer months.

The Sebastiani Vineyards and Winery date from 1904. Though distinctly younger than the Buena Vista Vaults they have, however, remained to this day in the ownership of the founder of the firm. There are conducted tours between 10 a.m. and 5 p.m.

Unlike Napa which is of no historical significance, Sonoma, which was in 1846 for a while capital of the State, has its place in the history of California. Mariano Guadelupe Vallejo, who was born in Monterey (see entry), then the capital of the Spanish colony of Alta California, became the Commander-in-Chief of the Mexican armed forces in the province after the Spanish yoke had been cast off. Between 1836 and 1846 he was the unchallenged ruler of North California which he governed from Sonoma.

Sonoma

More and more Americans flocked to the province, however, and on 14 June 1846 they took over Sonoma Barracks, arrested Vallejo and proclaimed an independent republic of

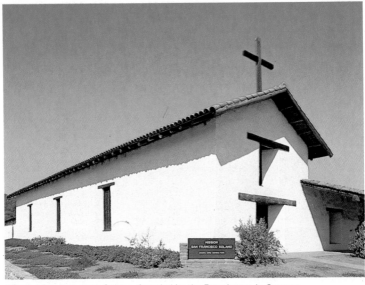

Mission San Francisco Solano, founded by the Franciscans in Sonoma

California. This had its own flag, with a bear as its emblem; it is still occasionally to be seen in California. Just a month later, however, US troops took control of the whole of Alta California, and that was an end of the dream of an independent republic here.

On the plaza in Sonoma what still remains of Vallejo's residence (the greater part of the house was destroyed by fire in 1867), has been restored to its 1840's appearance and is open to visitors (daily 10 a.m.–5 p.m.). Further on stands Adobe Barracks in which Vallejo's troops were quartered. In addition, the many 19th c. houses are worth seeing. Also in Sonoma is the Mission San Francisco Solano, the most northerly and last of the missions set up by the Franciscans along the Californian coast. It fulfilled its original function for a bare decade, from 1823 to 1833. Work on restoring the mission was begun in 1909, and archaeological investigations are still undertaken from time to time. (Open daily, 10 a.m.–5 p.m.)

Napa Valley

Napa lies at the entry into the valley of the same name which stretches away N to Calistoga, the site of California's "Old Faithful" geyser. Like its big counterpart in Yellowstone Park it belches out water regularly every 40 minutes, although its rhythm sometimes changes for unknown reasons; then about every four minutes it spews out boiling water but not to the normal height. Open daily, 9 a.m.–6 p.m. (5 p.m. in winter).

There are opportunities for going on tours around several wineries in the Napa Valley, and it is generally possible to

Vineyards in Napa Valley

One of the many wine vaults in Napa Valley

taste the wines, too. The wineries are clearly signposted. Special mention must be made of the Greystone Wineyards belonging to the Christian Brothers, a Catholic missionary order, the wineries of Charles Krug, founded in 1861 by a German and one of the oldest firms here, and Beaulieu, Inglenook and Sterling Vineyards. As regards the wines, Cabernet Sauvignon among the red and Johanisberg Riesling among the white are of particular note.

St Helena

For visitors to Napa Valley who are interested not only in wineries and vineyards, a short visit to the Silverado Museum in the small town of St Helena is to be recommended.

Here are displayed a number of interesting exhibits connected with the Scottish writer Robert Louis Stevenson. The museum is open daily, Mondays excepted, from noon until 4 p.m. (Free.)

Jack London State Park

Near the village of Glen Ellen, in Sonoma Valley, is the entrance to the Jack London State Park, named for the Californian author. Not far from the entrance is the "House of Happy Walls" built by his widow, and about a mile further on is the grave of this writer who lived only 40 years but found time to write 50 novels and innumerable short stories. Here, too, is the still-imposing ruin of Wolf House, built by London but burned down before it could be occupied.

National Maritime Museum Park   G7

Location
End of Polk Street in Aquatic Park

Bus routes
19, 30, 32, 47

Cable car
60

The National Maritime Museum illustrates the history of the seafarers and their ships which have made a vital contribuiton to the development of trade and population on the American West Coast. Ships dating back to the early history of California, the objects used by the seamen and other exhibits give a lively impression of the life and work of those who built and sailed the ships. The museum's departments occupy different sites.

National Maritime Museum

Opening times
Daily, 10 a.m.–5 p.m. (until 6 p.m. in summer)

Closed
New Year's Day
Christmas Day

Conducted tours
Daily 12.30 p.m., 3.30 p.m.

The building dates from 1939 and was used for a variety of purposes before being converted into the present National Maritime Museum a good dozen years later. It contains models of the different sorts of ships that frequently passed through the Golden Gate – passenger ships, freighters and men-of-war.

The upper floor has a collection of shop models, relics, old photographs, paintings, maps and sailors' handicrafts.

In addition, there is a library with a collection of West Coast shipping pictures in Building E (2nd Floor), Lower Fort Mason.

Six ships, all of which can be visited are moored at Hyde Street Pier.

View of the exterior of the National Maritime Museum

"Eureka", a ferry which was in operation from 1890 to 1957. It carried passengers between Marin County and Oakland. In its day it was the largest passenger ferry in the world. Propulsion was by means of paddles.

"C. A. Thayer" is a sailing schooner built in 1895. It was first used in the lumber trade, then carried salted salmon and finally, until 1950, was used for cod-fishing in the Bering Sea.

"Wapama", a steam schooner of 1915, was used in the lumber trade, but it also had cabins for passengers.

"Alma", a two-masted lighter, built in 1891 to carry coal, sand, lumber and hay in the bay and up the rivers flowing into it; in use until 1958.

"Hercules", a high-seas tug which hauled ships into the West Coast harbours during the period from 1907 to 1962.

"Balclutha" is a steel-hulled sailing vessel built in England in 1886. It was mainly used to carry coal round Cape Horn to San Francisco and corn back to Europe. It has been restored to its original state. (Visiting Mon.–Thurs. 9 a.m.–6 p.m. Sun. until 9 p.m.)

A US submarine (built 1943) which has seen action in the Pacific during the Second World War. Visiting June–Oct., daily 9 a.m.–9 p.m.; Nov.–May, Sun.–Thurs., 9 a.m.–6 p.m. (until 9 p.m. Fri. and Sat.). Entrance fee charged.

Location
Foot of Hyde Street, between Fisherman's Wharf and Aquatic Park

Opening times
Daily, 10 a.m.–5 p.m. (until 6 p.m. in summer)

Entrance fee charged

"Balclutha"

Mooring
Pier 43

USS "Pampanito"

Mooring: Pier 45 (Fisherman's Wharf)

99

The sailing vessel "Balclutha", restored for the National Maritime Museum

Navy/Marine Corps/Coast Guard Museum

Location
Treasure Island

Bus routes
AC Transit from Bus
Station, Mission Street and
1st Street; information
about departures: tel.
839–2882

Opening times
Daily 10 a.m.–3.30 p.m.

Closed: New Year,
Easter, Thanksgiving
and Christmas

The construction of the Navy/Marine Corps/Coast Guard Museum was begun at the time of the United States Bicentennial Celebrations. With displays, documents and pictures the museum illustrates the part played by the US Navy and Marine Corps in the Pacific. A special attraction is the huge mural by Lowell Nesbitt.

Wonderful views of the skyscrapers of San Francisco may be enjoyed during the drive over the San Francisco–Oakland Bridge and especially from Treasure Island. Treasure Island is, it must be added, a man-made island; that is to say, it is a part of Yerba Buena Island which was reclaimed from the sea. The project was carried out for the 1939 Golden Gate Exhibition. Free entry.

*Nob Hill   H8(I4/5)

Location
W of Chinatown

Cable car
61 (California Street)

Nob Hill, rising to more than 330 ft (100 m), is one of the smartest districts of San Francisco. Before the 1906 earthquake the most prosperous citizens lived here, and there are still many palatial homes to be seen.

Three explanations are offered for the name. It may be linked with the word "Nabob" which comes from India and means a rich man; or else with the word "snob"; or perhaps – and this seems most likely – with "knob" meaning a knoll or rounded hill.

On Nob Hill – the premises of the Pacific Union Club

Originally the area was called "California Street Hill", for the street leading up to it from the financial quarter. From the end of the 1850s the area began to attract the most prosperous citizens – bankers, industrialists and newspaper owners. They were followed some 15 to 20 years later by the railroad millionaires who had recently made their pile, including Charles Crocker, Leland Stanford, Mark Hopkins and Collis Huntingdon. They were "not sole proprietors of California, but they were able to represent its major interests" as one book about San Francisco puts it.

Among the buildings on Nob Hill the following are noteworthy:

Stouffer Stanford Court Hotel (905 California Street): originally a luxurious private residence built in 1911 and converted into a hotel in 1972. Stanford Villa stood here until the earthquake.

Mark Hopkins Inter-Continental Hotel (999 California Street): Hopkins Villa stood here until it was destroyed in the earthquake. It was not until 1925 that the 20-storey hotel was constructed. From its "Top of the Mark" bar there is one of the finest views out over the city.

Fairmont Hotel and Tower (950 Mason Street): it was paid for by James G. Fair, the "Silver King", and gutted by fire just before its opening in 1906. Consequently it took another year to complete.

The foyer may be regarded as one of the finest public rooms

101

in San Francisco. The exterior lift in the tower added in 1962 is a special attraction.

Pacific Union Club (1000 California Street): San Francisco's most exclusive club for gentlemen, it occupies the villa built in 1886 for James Flood, another "Silver King", and renovated 26 years later.

University Club (800 Powell Street), on the corner of California Street and originally Stanford's stables: it was built in 1912 as a sort of Florentine town mansion.

Grace Cathedral (see entry)

Masonic Memorial Auditorium (1111 California Street): one of the few modern buildings to have been erected here, it dates from 1958. There are several Art Deco houses from the 1920s – 1250 Jones Street, 1298 Sacramento Street, 1000 Mason Street, and 1100 Sacramento Street.

Huntington Park (California Street) between the Pacific Union Club and Grace Cathedral (see entry), is on land given to the city by Collis Huntington's widow in 1915. It is now one of the most beautiful small parks in San Francisco.

North Beach (Amusement Area)   H/17/8(I/J3/4)

Location
Broadway, Columbus
Avenue, Washington
Square

Bus route
15

North Beach is one of the most bustling parts of San Francisco where immigrant peoples from all four corners of the globe are to be seen on the streets. The name is deceptive in so far as there is no beach whatever to be seen here.

The most important attractions of North Beach are reached by continuing further along Grant Avenue, the main street of Chinatown (see entry). North Beach starts beyond Columbus Avenue and Broadway. This is the place to enjoy San Francisco's night life – and it goes on pretty well 24 hours a day – for the entertainments with their bright lights and advertisements are open virtually without interruption. Women dance and cavort in various states of undress, and there are pornographic cinemas and live theatre shows. There are also jazz clubs which regularly feature famous jazz musicians.

There are also a number of discos famous throughout the city in this district. At the corner of Kearny and Columbus Streets there is an especially fine view of the Transamerica Pyramid (see entry). But North Beach is more than a night spot. Further along Columbus Avenue lies Washington Square, the centre of the Italian quarter where there is perhaps more local colour than in the "Little Italys" of other American cities. More than 50,000 Italians live here, and a glance at the shops and restaurants is enough to persuade any visitor that the Italian way of life is still practised in this area. Italians have perhaps played a larger part in the history of San Francisco than any other European ethnic group.

Telegraph Hill with Coit Tower (see entries) is also a part of North Beach.

North Beach – San Francisco's night-time playground

Oakland (Town and Harbour)   I32

At the E end of the San Francisco–Oakland Bridge (see
entry) lies Oakland on hilly ground that rises to 1750 ft (533
m). It is an industrial town that was founded in 1850. Its
population is now about 330,000. Oakland is the largest
town on the E side of San Francisco Bay. It has overtaken
San Francisco as the most important harbour in North California and has more industry, with several large shipyards,
about 1600 factories and the termini of important railroads.
Oakland has a black population amounting to 36%, which is
particularly high for the W part of the USA, and it is here that
the militant Black Panthers originated.
Rivalry between San Francisco and Oakland is keen, and the
jokes made by the inhabitants about their counterparts in
the other city have nothing kindly about them. Oakland has
not, however, got very much to offer sightseers.

Location
7 miles (12 km) NE

Underground station
BART (Station Lake Merritt)

Bus route
AC Transit Line A

In the centre of the town is Lake Merritt, a 150-acre salt-
water lagoon on which boating is allowed. Not far from the
lagoon, which is surrounded by Lakeside Park, there is
Children's Fairyland (fee) and a Japanese Garden. Oakland
Museum (see below) is set in large grounds at the SW end
of Lake Merritt.

Lake Merritt

Devotees of the author Jack London (see Introduction –
Famous People) will want to visit Jack London Square. The
bust of the Californian author which stands there is,
however, less interesting than "Heinold's First and Last

Jack London's Waterfront
Location
Jack London Square (foot
of Broadway)

103

Oakland

The only museum devoted exclusively to California: Oakland Museum

Sculpture by a Californian artist: Fletcher Benton's "M"

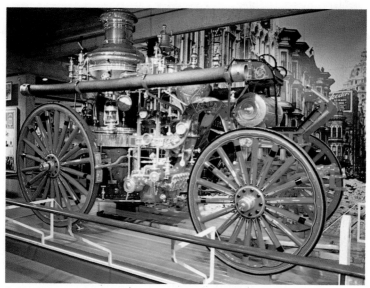

Oakland Museum – an exhibit from the Department of Californian History . . .

Chance Saloon''; London did not go there just to drink but also to write.
There is also London's Yukon cabin, and ''The Village'' – a themed shopping complex adjacent to the square.

Tourists in Oakland on the first or third Saturday in the month should not fail to visit the Paramount Theater of the Arts (2025 Broadway). It is no less than one of the last Art Deco picture houses from the 1920s in the United States which can still be seen. At 10 a.m. on the first and third Saturday of each month (except holidays) there are conducted tours of this building which was designed by the architect Timothy L. Pflueger. The Oakland Symphony Orchestra now gives concerts here.

Paramount Theater of the Arts

*Oakland Museum

Oakland Museum stands SW of Lake Merritt. It has notable collections illustrating Californian natural history, history and folk customs. It is set in extensive grounds where visitors can stroll.
The origins of this museum go back to 1910 when the Oakland Public Museum was created, to be followed a few years later by the Oakland Art Gallery. The present museum, which is almost entirely below ground, was designed by the well-known architect Kevin Roche. It is the only museum devoted exclusively to the history and culture of San Francisco.
This limitation in range was originally dictated primarily by

Address
1000 Oak Street

Opening times
Wed.–Sat. 10 a.m.–5 p.m.;
Sun. noon–7 p.m.

Closed
Mon. and Tue.

Entry free

. . . and the "Frank Pierce Memorial Window" by Arthur F. Mathews

economic factors, for Oakland could not compete with other museums for the purchase of expensive pictures.

The upper storey, through which visitors enter the museum, is devoted to works by Californian painters.

Underneath is a great exhibition gallery concerned with Californian history. The lowest floor – this designation is not entirely accurate as the storeys are arranged below one another as in terraces – is devoted to the natural history of California. There is an auditorium down here, too.

As well as Californian painters, photographers are well represented, among them Ansel Adams, Dorothea Lange, Edward Weston and Edward Muybridge.

Octagon House   G8

Address
2645 Gough Street, corner
Union Street

Bus route 41

Conducted tours
Every 2nd Sun. and 2nd
and 4th Thurs. of the
month, noon–3 p.m..
Donation suggested.

Closed
January and holidays

In the late 1850s there was a short-lived vogue in San Francisco for octagonal houses with dormer windows and domes. It was triggered off by a book that recommended this design as making for a healthier life style. Just two of these octagonal houses remain, however, and only Octagon House, which was built in 1861, can still be visited.

Octagon House is undoubtedly a curiosity. It serves now as the Californian headquarters of the National Society of Colonial Dames in America.

The objects on display date from the American colonial period before the founding of San Francisco and are somewhat of an anachronism here.

A curiosity as a museum – Octagon House ▶

The Old Mint – one of the buildings that withstood the 1906 earthquake

Old Mint

19(I6)

Address
5th Street and Mission
Street

Opening times
Mon.–Fri. 10 a.m.–4 p.m.

Closed
Sat., Sun. and Public
holidays

Conducted tours
Every ½ hour until 3 p.m.

Free entry

This building was put up between 1873 and 1874. It was one of the few in the Mission Street area that not only withstood the 1906 earthquake but was not even damaged. Several rooms have been restored to the appearance they had in the 19th c. The most noteworthy is the office of the Mint's Director.

Among the exhibits is a pyramid constructed of gold bars (valued at $5 million) in a circular safe, many privately minted coins from the early days of San Francisco, photographs and works of art. There are also temporary exhibitions from time to time. Each visitor can mint for himself a souvenir medal on a coin press dating from 1869.

Old St Mary's Church

See Chinatown

Pacific Film Archive

See Berkeley, University Art Museum

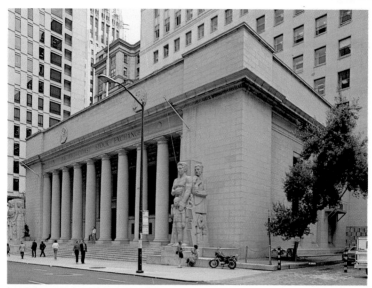

Buildings of the Pacific Stock Exchange

Pacific Stock Exchange

I8(J5)

Founded in 1873, the Pacific Stock Exchange now occupies buildings designed by the architects Miller and Pflueger and erected in 1930. The exuberant decoration bears witness to the date of construction. The sculptures are by Ralph Stackpole.

During trading hours it is possible to go into the gallery and watch at close quarters the hectic activity of the stockbrokers. Visitors are required to have a recommendation from a San Francisco stockbroking firm.

Address
301 Pine Street

*Pier 39 (Shopping and Amusement Centre)

H7

Quite near Fisherman's Wharf (see entry) a complex with 100 shops and numerous restaurants was created on the site of a disused pier. Since its inauguration in 1978 it has been a great attraction. Pier 39 was completely reconstructed, using timbers from old ships and tearing down other piers in the vicinity in order to provide moorings for small boats.

On the ground floor and upper storey of this more than 1000 ft (305 m) long pier all is activity and bustle. At virtually all hours of the day there are performances of one sort or another. From the end of the pier, and also from the restaurant jutting right out over the bay, there are lovely views of the skyscrapers of San Francisco. The film (movie) "San

Location
Embarcadero

Bus routes
19, 30

Cable car
59

109

Pier 39 – a disused pier converted into a shopping and amusement centre

Francisco Experience" is shown here, complete with simulations of the 1906 and 1989 earthquakes. It is also the departure point for 1¼-hour cruises of the bay (tel. 781–7877).

Pioneer Hall (Museum)   G9

Address
456 McAllister Street

Opening times
All year (except Aug.):
Mon.–Fri. 10 a.m.–4 p.m.

Closed
Aug. and Public holidays

Entry free

The Society of Californian Pioneers has a museum and a library in Pioneer Hall (near Civic Center – see entry). The main object of concern is the early history of California, before 1869. As well as historical coaches there are historical documents and objects on display and a Children's Gallery of Californian history.
A comprehensive library on the topic and a large collection of photographs are available for research by those interested in the history of California.

Presidio (Park and Museum)   E8

Location
In the NW of the city at the Golden Gate (main entrance: Lombard and Lyon Streets)

The name "Presidio" goes back to 1776 when Spanish troops were first quartered on this site. This wooded stretch of land which covers just under 1½ sq. miles (4 sq. km) and is criss-crossed by roads lies on the northern extremity of the San Francisco peninsula, jutting out into the Pacific. It is at present the headquarters of the United States 6th Army.

St Mary's Cathedral, one of the most impressive churches in the city . . .

. . . with a cross and baldacchino made out of 7000 aluminium rods

St Mary's Cathedral

Bus route
45 to end of line at Lyon
and Greenwich

Tours
tel. 561–3870 in advance

Flag parade
daily 5 p.m.

In the park, to most of which the public is allowed free access and from which there are fine views, stands the Officers' Club. Dating from 1776 it is the only relic of Spanish days.

The National Military Cemetery is also part of the Presidio. It has a burial ground where lie more than 15,000 who died in the First World War. Also noteworthy is the gravestone of "Pauline Tyler, Union Spy". She was an actress who served as a Union spy in the course of the American Civil War, winning promotion to the rank of major.

The grounds also include Fort Point National Historic Site (see entry).

Presidio Army Museum

The Presidio Army Museum is housed in an old military hospital dating from 1860s. There are exhibitions of relics and documents which illustrate the part played by the military in the development of San Francisco. In the grounds stand two restored "earthquake" cottages, having been moved from their original sites. (Open Tues.–Sun. 10 a.m.– 4 p.m.; closed Thanksgiving, Christmas and New Year; entry free.)

---

*St Mary's Cathedral   G9

Location
Gough Street and Geary
Street

Bus route
38 (do not take 38L, limited
bus)

Opening times
Mon.–Sun. 6.45 a.m.–
5 p.m. Sun. and public
holidays, afternoons only

St Mary's Cathedral, the third to bear this name, is by far the most impressive of all the churches in San Francisco. No tourist should omit it from his itinerary.

After the second cathedral on Van Ness Avenue had been burnt down in 1962 the construction of a new one was undertaken. It is on a site formerly occupied by a supermarket.

The building was designed by the architects Angus McSweeney, Paul A. Ryan and John M. Lee of San Francisco, Pietro Belluschi of the Massachusetts Institute of Technology in Cambridge, near Boston, and Pier Luigi Nervi of Rome. It has a nave without pillars and a dome 195 ft (59 m) high in which 7 ft (2 m) stained-glass windows like great translucent pathways come together at the top to form a multi-coloured cross. The four windows in the dome symbolise the elements, fire (W), air (N), water (E), and earth (S).

The altar, at which the celebrant faces the congregation in accord with the recommendations of the Vatican Council of 1962, is surrounded by rows of seats on three sides. Above it hangs a cross and a baldacchino made out of 7000 aluminium rods perpetually on the move. The organ, built by the brothers Ruffati in Padua, stands on a plinth, giving a sculptural effect.

The church's open attitude towards the outside world is symbolised by great glass windows through which the church and the city seem to be able to grow into one another.

The view to the SW, with Twin Peaks (see entry), San Francisco's second highest hills, in the centre, is especially impressive.

A school with three courtyards, a large auditorium and a council chamber form part of the cathedral complex.

San Francisco African-American Historical and Cultural Society (Museum)   G7

The only museum devoted to the culture and history of the blacks W of the Mississippi is in San Francisco.

Permanent exhibits always on show include documents and pictures relative to the history of the blacks in California and the part played by blacks in the American Civil War of 1861–5.

Temporary exhibitions of works by black artists, especially those working in and around San Francisco, are regularly mounted.

Guided tours can be arranged on request in advance (tel. 441–0640). Entry Free.

Address
Fort Mason, Building C.
Marina Boulevard

Bus route
41, 47

Opening times
Wed.–Sun. noon–5 p.m.

Closed
Sun., Mon. and Public holidays

San Francisco Fire Department Pioneer Memorial Museum   F9

Behind the massive doors of the museum – should they be shut, visitors should ring the bell at the fire station – is kept a remarkable collection of photographs, equipment and documents that come from the various fire brigades of San Francisco, especially the Volunteer Fire Brigade which was in existence from 1849 to 1866.

Much space is given over to documents concerning events during the disastrous blaze following the 1906 earthquake. There is a special exhibition devoted to Lillie Hitchcock Coit who paid for the erection of Coit Tower on Telegraph Hill (see entry) as a memorial in honour of the fire brigade and was herself made an honorary member of the fire brigade.

Address
655 Presidio Avenue

Bus route
38

Opening times
Thur.–Sun. 1–4 p.m.

Closed
Mon.–Wed. Public holidays

Entry free

San Francisco Museum of Modern Art

See Civic Center

*San Francisco–Oakland Bay Bridge   J/K8

This bridge links the city with Oakland (see entry) and the towns on the E side of the bay. It was opened in 1936, six months before the Golden Gate Bridge (see entry). The bridge is 8 miles (14 km) long, which makes it one of the longest steel bridges in the world. It consists of two interconnected suspension bridges on the San Francisco side, a tunnel through the island of Yerba Buena and a lattice-work bridge on the Oakland side.

The bridge has not quite the same dramatic aspect as the Golden Gate Bridge. But there is an especially fine view of it from the quay where the ferries depart for Sausalito (see entry) and Larkspur, on the right-hand side of the tower of the Ferry Building (see entry).

During the October 1989 earthquake the 50-year-old bridge revealed itself not to be 'quake-proof, its massive concrete construction serving merely to intensify the shock waves. A 50 ft/15 m section of the bridge collapsed burying several cars beneath the debris. A thorough renovation is planned.

Toll
Westbound only, $1

1989 earthquake

One of the longest steel bridges in the world, San Francisco's Oakland Bay Bridge

San Francisco Zoo   B13

Location
Sloat Avenue and 45th
Avenue

Underground station
MUNI Metro L

Opening times
Daily 10 a.m.–5 p.m.

Entry fee charged

San Francisco did not begin to lay out its zoo until quite late (1929), but now it is one of the six most important in the United States. Its designers took the Hagenbeck Zoo at Hamburg-Stellingen as their model. The chief attractions are the snow leopards, polar bears, elephants, pigmy hippos, white rhinos and the monkeys which inhabit an island of their own. The "Primate Discovery Center", using computer technology and participatory techniques to explain about its resident monkeys, was added in 1985, while "Gorilla World" (costing $2 million) is one of the world's largest gorilla habitats.

There is also a children's zoo here which is open slightly shorter hours than the zoo. Children are able to play with young animals and to feed them. They can also go for rides on giant tortoises and on roundabouts.

*Sausalito (Fishing Village)   H32

Location
8 miles (13 km) N

Bus routes
Golden Gate Bus from
Market Street and
7th Street

Sausalito takes its name from the Spanish for "little willows", but there are no willows to be found there. There are, however, many other things to see in this old fishing village on the N end of the Golden Gate Bridge – narrow winding lanes which are partially interconnected by wooden stairways, a large colony of houseboats and island residences

A characteristic sight at Sausalito: the houseboat colony

Spreckels' Mansion, built in the French Baroque style

Ferries
From S wing of the Ferry
Building (tel. 332–6600); or
from Pier 41, Fisherman's
Wharf (tel. 546–BOAT)

which for years have been a sort of emblem of Sausalito;
interesting boutiques and bazaars, good restaurants and
an atmosphere even livelier than that of San Francisco.
Since the construction of the Golden Gate Bridge (see
entry) Sausalito has become a suburb of San Francisco, and
many of its 6500 permanent inhabitants are commuters.
The main streets of the village are Bridgeway and Princess
Street. Nearly all the shops and restaurants are here, along
with little hotels and motels.
Apart from the friendly atmosphere, for which Sausalito is
famous, there is one of the finest views of San Francisco
whether the city is still lying enshrouded in early morning
mist with only the tops of the skyscrapers standing out
above it or whether you look across on a clear day towards
the residential quarters of San Francisco, behind which the
tall buildings of the centre rise up high so that old and new
San Francisco can be seen all together. Sausalito is in any
event well worth a visit.

Sigmund Stern Grove (Amphitheatre)   C13

Location
Sloat Boulevard and
19th Avenue

Underground station
MUNI L to Sunset
Boulevard, then change
and take No. 18 bus

Sigmund Stern Grove is a natural amphitheatre in the midst
of conifer and eucalyptus woods. Each year from mid-June
to mid-August at 2 p.m. on Sundays free musical performances are given here – concerts, operettas, musicals,
occasionally opera and ballet. These performances are very
popular, and they can be recommended to visitors to San
Francisco.
Pine Lake Park lies close by; it is possible to picnic there,
too, also with facilities for lawn bowling, croquet or putting.

Skyscrapers

San Francisco's ten tallest buildings all stand in the business quarter. Outside this area no more skyscrapers will be
allowed, and it is doubtful whether the city authorities will
permit any building taller than the Transamerica Pyramid
(see entry) even in the business quarter.

1. Transamerica Pyramid, 600 Montgomery Street	853 ft (260 m)
2. Bank of America, 555 California Street	761 ft (231 m)
3. First Interstate Center, 345 California Street	712 ft (217 m)
4. 101 California Street	591 ft (180 m)
5. 5 Fremont Center, 50 Fremont Street	591 ft (180 m)
6. Citicorp Center, 1 Sansome Street	587 ft (179 m)
7. One Embarcadero Center	568 ft (173 m)
8. Four Embarcadero Center	568 ft (173 m)
9. One Market Plaza	565 ft (172 m)
10. Wells Fargo Building, 44 Montgomery Street	561 ft (171 m)

Sonoma and Sonoma Valley

See Napa and Sonoma Valleys

Spreckels' Mansion   G8

This mansion is in the Pacific Heights quarter of the city, two
blocks away from Van Ness Street. It is worthy of attention
on account of the man who had it built, Adolph B. Spreckels,
son of Claus Spreckels, an immigrant from Hanover who
became the "sugar king" of California, and also because of
its architecture. It is one of the buildings designed by the
architect George Applegarth and it is constructed on the
lines of a French Baroque palace.

Applegarth used white stone for this building which occupies the space of half a block. Three years later, in 1915, he
was commissioned by Spreckels to build in Lincoln Park the
California Palace of the Legion of Honor (see entry) which
he had given to the city. Twenty-seven rooms are now
available for tourists (tel. 861–3008).

Address
2080 Washington Street (in
Lafayette Park)

Bus route
48

*Stanford University Museum of Art

This museum, like the university itself, owes its creation to
the generosity of Leland A. Stanford, one of the richest men
in San Francisco. He was, for instance, President of the
Central Pacific Railroad, Governor of California and a
United States Senator. In 1887 Stanford had a college built
on his farm at Palo Alto. This developed into today's important university. The museum followed a few years later.
Both were memorials to Stanford's son who died at the age
of 16 and who had begun to collect mainly archaeological
artefacts during his childhood. In the museum are re-
constructions of the two rooms which he occupied in his
father's house at Nob Hill (see entry).

The museum was opened in 1894 but completed only in
1905. It is modelled on the National Museum of Athens and
has an Ionic colonnade, marble corridors and large exhibition galleries. Stanford and, after his death, his widow purchased major collections for the museum.

There are, for instance, hundreds of archaeological objects
from Cyprus (from the Metropolitan Museum in New York),
a collection of Indian burial offerings (from an exhibition in
New Orleans), and the great collection of Japanese and
Chinese art which formerly was in the possession of Baron
Ikeda. (Since the time of that acquisition the Far Eastern
collection has increased to more than 7000 objects.) The
Stanford family collection of American paintings of the
West (William Keith, Thomas Hill and Charles Nahl) has also
come into the museum which in the past 20 years has been
trying to concentrate its buying on European art of the last
two centuries. Consequently important works from this
period up to Paul Klee are now on show.

Distance
33 miles (53 km) (Highway
101)

Opening times
Tues.–Fri. 10 a.m.–
5 p.m.; Sat.–Sun.
1 p.m.–5 p.m.

One of San Francisco's 43 hills: Telegraph Hill, showing Coit Tower

The motif of the series of murals in the Coit Tower: working life in California

The museum works in close co-operation with the art history department of the university, and students are given the opportunity of examining at close quarters objects connected with their particular special study.

Strybing Arboretum (Botanical Garden)

See Golden Gate Park

Telegraph Hill   I7(J3)

Telegraph Hill rises 295 ft (90 m) on the N side of the inner city. It is one of San Francisco's 43 hills. Rather like Montmartre in Paris, it has many artists' studios on its slopes as well as villas for the well-to-do middle classes.

Bus route
39 from Washington Square, or Bay and Taylor Streets in the Fisherman's Wharf area

It is often said that San Francisco, like Rome and Lisbon, is a "city built on seven hills", but that refers only to the most important, among which Telegraph Hill is counted (the other six are Nob Hill (see entry), Rincon Hill, the Twin Peaks (see entry), Russian Hill, Lone Mountain and Mount Davidson).

There is at present no telegraphic installation on Telegraph Hill, but the name goes back to the so-called semaphore station erected on what was then a barren hilltop at the time of the Gold Rush. From this tower signals were sent to the merchants in Yerba Buena Cove, the present-day finance quarter, when ships were coming in through the Golden Gate. This enabled the merchants to get to the anchorages even before the ships had made fast and start trading without losing a moment. The signal tower was, however, operative for only a few years.

*Coit Tower

Coit Tower stands 500 ft (152 m) above sea-level on the top of Telegraph Hill. It has mural paintings which are worth a visit. It is also one of the best vantage points from which to view San Francisco, though it is not quite so high as the Twin Peaks (see entry). There is a lift up to the viewing terrace at 210 ft (64 m), which is glazed with Perspex. In clear weather it is possible to see as far as Mount Tamalpais (see entry).

Opening times
Daily: June–Sept., 10 a.m.–5.30 p.m.; Oct.– May, 9 a.m.–4.30 p.m.

Closed
Thanksgiving, Christmas and New Year

Entry fee charged

The name "Coit Tower" recalls Lillie Hitchcock Coit (1843–1929), an honorary member of a fire fighting company. She bequeathed $125,000 for the erection of a tower in honour of the fire brigade. The architect Arthur Brown jr. who was also responsible for the City Hall (see Civic Center) and other public buildings constructed it in 1934. It takes the form of a free-standing column in which many claim they can recognise the valve of a fire hose.

The inside of the tower is decorated with 16 monumental murals, the work of 25 painters and their 19 assistants. They were undertaken as part of the work creation scheme designed to alleviate the Great Depression.

The theme of the cycle of pictures is working life in California in 1934. The largest (34 by 10 ft – 10 by 3 m) mural was painted by Ralph Stackpole and depicts the industries of California. Like most of the other murals it shows strong influence by Diego de Rivera, the Mexican artist who resided for a while in San Francisco in the 1930s. Apart from the murals at ground-level, those inside the tower can only be viewed on Saturday mornings from 11 a.m.

Coit Tower is surrounded by Pioneer Park. This was a stony barren hillside until it was laid out as a park when the Centennial Celebrations of the United States took place on Telegraph Hill. The bronze statue of Christopher Columbus is especially noteworthy; the plinth was a gift of the city of Genoa.

Pioneer Park

Tiburon (Fishing Village)   H31

Tiburon, which is situated on a peninsula with the same name, still retains, like Sausalito (see entry), much that recalls its past as a fishing village. The wooden houses in the major thoroughfare (Main Street) are now occupied by smart shops, such as boutiques, antique dealers and galleries, and the fish restaurants offer excellent fare. The narrow up-and-down streets lead into the modern part of Tiburon where the villas of the well-to-do citizens are to be found. Just like Sausalito, Tiburon seems to be much further than a mere 15 miles (24 km) from San Francisco (the ferry crossing amounts to only half that distance). It is like being in a different world.

Location
15 miles (24 km) NE
(Highway 101)

Ferry
Daily departures from Pier 43½, Fisherman's Wharf
(tel. 456–BOAT for schedule)

**Transamerica Pyramid (Skyscraper)   I8(J5)

Since its completion in 1972 the Transamerica Pyramid which can be seen virtually everywhere in San Francisco has become the new symbol of the city. It is situated in the middle of the financial quarter and, with its 48 storeys, it reaches up 853 ft (260 m) into the sky. It belongs to an insurance company which occupies a third of the total office space. This skyscraper is of a unique design, and there is nothing else quite like it in the world. The architect of this building, with its 200 ft (61 m) high hollow spire which is illuminated from within, was William Pereira of Los Angeles. The sides of the pyramidal spire are clad with aluminium sheeting. The whole building has 6000 windows.
On the E side of the building, on Clay Street, there is a small park in which 80 of the famous Californian Redwood trees (see Muir Woods) have been planted. It is open to the public during usual business hours.
Close by stands the Bank Exchange Saloon. It occupies the site of the Montgomery Block which was demolished in 1959. When it was built 106 years earlier it was the first major office complex in San Francisco.

Address
600 Montgomery Street

Opening times
Viewing Chamber, Mon.–Fri. 8 a.m.–4 p.m.

◀ *New symbol of San Francisco – the Transamerica Pyramid*

View from the Twin Peaks down over the city and bay of San Francisco

---

*Twin Peaks
F12

Location
Off Twin Peaks Boulevard

Underground/Bus
MUNI K, L or M to Forest Hill; change to 36 bus (northbound), exit at Skyview and Marview

These are two 900 ft (274 m) hills, the one to the S being 6 ft (2 m) taller than its neighbour. They are not, in fact, the highest of San Francisco's 43 hills, a distinction belonging to Mount Davidson which is some 30 ft (9 m) higher. But they are easier of access and offer what is perhaps the finest views out over the city and the bay.

The easiest way to get there is by the motor road up to the summit, but public transport can also be used by those prepared to tackle a rather steep, though quite short foot-path. No. 37 buses go up to Parkridge and Crestline, and then the driver will point out the way.

The summit is the only one in San Francisco which has not been built over or at least laid out as gardens but remains in its original state. From it the observer can look down over San Francisco and the bay.

There is nowhere better than this from which to appreciate the vastness of the city. The Spaniards called the twin hills "Los pechos de la Chola" (i.e. the Breasts of the Indian Maiden).

Even on warm days strong cool breezes blow in here from the Pacific, especially in the late afternoon. Warm clothing is, therefore, recommended.

What must be the most unusual building in San Francisco: the Vedanta Temple ▶

Union Square – centre point of a city that really has no centre

Union Square

19(I5)

Location
Powell, Stockton, Geary
and Post Streets

Cable Car
59

San Francisco really has no central point, but Union Square comes nearest to fulfilling this function. It is here or in the immediate vicinity that numerous lines of communication come together, and here are to be found important shops (Macy's, Magnin, Neiman-Marcus, Saks Fifth Avenue) and hotels (Grand Hyatt San Francisco, Westin St Francis, Sir Francis Drake); the most important theatres are just a short step away, in Geary Street, and the SW corner of the square, where Geary Street and Powell Street meet, is reckoned to be the liveliest spot in all San Francisco. Only three blocks S in Market Street (see entry) stand the Cable Car Museum (see entry) and the city's information office.

The site of Union Square was presented to the city by its first American Mayor, John W. Geary. Its ornamental palm trees are unique in central San Francisco. Beneath the square there has been a vast underground car park since 1942. Union Square received its name during the American Civil War (1861–5) when mass demonstrations took place here in favour of the troops of the Northern Union and against the secessionist Southern States.

In 1902 a Corinthian column of granite with a bronze goddess of victory was erected here in commemoration of Admiral George Dewey's triumph in the Bay of Manila during the short Spanish-American War of 1898.

Political demonstrations still take place in Union Square, but the benches are mainly occupied all day long while the weather is warm by strollers and poor people from the slums S of Market Street (see entry).

Vedanta Temple   G8

This building is situated in Cow Hollow (see entry). It is described in the best-known architectural guide to San Francisco as "surely the most unusual" building in the city. It was built in 1905 by the architect Joseph A. Leonard. He worked in close collaboration with Swami Trigunatitananda who had founded, five years before, the Vedanta Society of North California which is still in existence. In its all but grotesque mixture of numerous styles – Queen Anne, Colonial, Oriental, Moorish and medieval – the building is supposed to symbolise the Vedanta concept that all religions are but ways of approaching the one God. Vedanta is the highest of the six systems in the Hindu philosophy of religion.

A crenellated European castle tower on one side is especially noteworthy, as is an octagonal cupola such as is raised above a Shiva temple on the other. Between them there is a double dome of the sort seen on Bengali temples.

Location
2963 Webster Street
(corner of Filbert Street)

Bus route
41

*Victorian Houses

Architecturally the physiognomy of San Francisco is characterised by the skyscrapers (see entry) of the city centre and by the wooden houses dating mainly from the 19th c.

The city takes its character from "Victorian Houses" as well as from skyscrapers

125

Victorian Houses

Skyline of San Francisco

in the residential quarters which, on account of the date of their construction, are generally called "Victorian Houses". The finest which were built between 1870 and 1906 were destroyed in the earthquake, especially those in Nob Hill and Van Ness Avenue. There still remain, however, more than 13,000 of these houses in various quarters – Bernal Heights, Duboce Triangle, Eureka, Glen Park, Haight-Ashbury, Mission District, Noe Valley, Potrero Hill and Western Addition.

Many have already been restored, and the renovation of the others will surely be undertaken in the next few years. It must, however, not be forgotten that about half of the wooden houses that have remained have been altered with new façades of asbestos sheeting, plaster and stone.

Italian Style

Between 1870 and 1880 narrow-guttered houses with arched façades were built in the Italian style which was so-called because details were imitated from Roman decorative styles.

San Francisco "Stick"

In the 1880s this vertical style developed into the San Francisco "Stick", differentiated from the simpler East Coast and Middle West "Stick". The designation derives from the fact that the vertical structure is stressed and the exterior decoration of the house is like a bundle of sticks. The term did not come into existence until after the houses had been built; it was the American architect Vincent Scully who first coined it. Stick houses, too, have arched façades, often crowned by a gable and with a cheap version of a dormer-window. It was at this time, too, that the habit started of painting the houses in light colours, a custom which has been revived for some of the restored houses.

In the 1890s the Queen Anne style developed. It is seen in more expensive houses, often free-standing, with towers added on and conical cupolas, loft gables and mass-produced ornamentation.

Queen Anne style

In the construction of all these houses use was made of the Redwood readily available near San Francisco. It was cheap, durable and fairly resistant to fire and insect damage.

Especially fine examples of houses of this sort are still to be seen today in the E part of Union Street and the thoroughfares in the vicinity, that is roughly from Gough Street to Divisidero Street (also Cow Hollow – see entry). There are also very attractive houses around Alamo Park, but the warning has to be given that this is a district unsafe for tourists. It is unwise to go there on foot, and even when travelling by automobile care should be taken.

San Francisco has only a few so-called Cast-iron houses. They can be identified by the stanchions on all floors, both inside and outside.

Cast-iron Houses

Perhaps the best known of these buildings in San Francisco is Columbus Tower (920 Kearny Street, on corner of Columbus Avenue). It dates from 1907. It is painted green and stands out in a district where all the other buildings are low structures. Nowadays people like to photograph it with the Transamerica Pyramid (see entry) in the background; the contrast in styles is remarkable.

War Memorial Opera House

See Civic Center

*Wells Fargo History Museum   l8(J5)

The Wells Fargo Bank building (main entrance in Montgomery Street) which was put up in 1959 is not itself of particular interest. But its museum is a rich source of information for all who wish to learn about the history of California from the Gold Rush era to the early 1900s.

Address
420 Montgomery Street

Opening times
Mon.–Fri. 9 a.m.–5 p.m.

Closed
Bank holidays

Entry free

Here may be seen an especially fine example of a so-called Concord coach. The name comes from the town of Concord in the State of New Hampshire where coaches of this sort were built. It was in 1852 that the Wells Fargo Express Co. was founded in San Francisco by Henry Wells from Vermont and William Fargo from New York. The firm used Concord coaches to transport passengers and freight, especially gold. There are relics of the Gold Rush and also exhibitions recalling the hard life of the "Forty-Niners".

A special display is devoted to Black Bart. In a period of just eight years, from about 1877 to 1885, he ambushed 28 coaches on his own. He often used to leave comic verses at the scene of the crime in which he claimed to be a sort of Robin Hood who robbed the rich so that he could give their possessions to the poor.

There is a comprehensive library open to anybody who is interested.

World of Oil, Chevron (Museum of Oil)   I8(J5)

Address
555 Market Street

Opening times
Mon.–Fri. 9 a.m.–4 p.m.

Closed
Public holidays

Entry free

This museum in the Standard Oil Company of California building will fascinate anybody interested in the story of oil from its discovery to the development of its countless by-products.

Everything is made clear to visitors by means of models of the equipment used in the oil-fields and three dioramas. There is also an 18-minute multi-media show called "Magic of a Refinery" which is put on several times each day. It calls for no fewer than 26 projectors.

**Yosemite National Park

Location
210 miles (354 km) SE in the Sierra Nevada (via Highway 120 from NW or 140 from SW)

Information
Tel. (209) 372–0264

Note
Hotel bookings in advance essential

Yosemite (pronounced Yossémmitty) is the second oldest National Park (after Yellowstone) in the United States. It is certainly worth a visit, especially if you happen already to have come as far as San Francisco. In theory the trip there and back can be fitted into a single day whether you travel in your own car or by bus. But this really does impose a strain, and to get to know Yosemite just reasonably well takes at least three days.

It is essential to book hotel accommodation in advance throughout the year, but particularly in the period from June to September when the tourist season is at its peak. All accommodation bookings are centrally organised

Worth the journey – Yosemite National Park with Cathedral Rocks and Merced River

(Ahwahnee Hotel, Wawona Hotel, Yosemite Lodge, Curry Village, and Yosemite West Cottages and Vacation Home Rentals). For any of these you need call only one number: (209) 252–4848.

History

The Yosemite area in the Sierra Nevada which covers an area of more than 1000 sq. miles (2590 sq. km) was declared a US National Park in 1890. It had been made a Californian State Park as early as 1864, during the American Civil War. White men discovered Yosemite Valley, amounting to only about 7 sq. miles (18 sq. km) of the present park in 1851, when members of a State battalion broke through into the valley while pursuing Indians, after white men sieving for gold in the foothills had been subjected to ambushes on many occasions. They did not in fact succeed in capturing the Indians but they reported back to the outside world that the Yosemite Valley was quite astonishingly beautiful. It takes its name from the Indian word "u-zu-ma-ta", referring to the grey bears found in the area.

The first expedition on horseback came in along Indian tracks in 1855. Others followed soon afterwards. In order to prevent private interests from spoiling the valley, Congress passed a law obliging the new State of California to protect the valley and the groves of Redwood (see Muir Park) at Mariposa.

A decade later the first roads into the valley were constructed. As early as 1877 coach journeys through it were being organised. In 1880 the area passed into the care of the Federal authorities and gradually was extended until it reached its present size. It was in 1900 that the first automobile was seen in Yosemite Valley, and in 1907 a railroad was constructed. It reached El Portal (on the W boundary of the park) and survived until 1945. In 1926 the all-weather Merced highway was built; it remains the most popular route.

There is, of course, not enough space to describe here in detail the many beauties of this National Park. The Merced River flows through Yosemite Valley which is situated at an altitude of about 4000 ft (1219 m). Massive granite cliffs rise in places another 4250 ft (1295 m) above that.

3000 ft (914 m) above the valley towers El Capitan in the great bulk of which so far no fissure has been discovered. On the opposite side the Three Brothers dominate the valley, as well as 8500 ft (2590 m) high Eagle Peak, Sentinel Rock, the two "cathedral spires" first scaled only some 50 years ago and Half Dome, this monolith being all that remains of a vast mass of rock, the other half having been swept away during the Ice Age. Some of these peaks are visible from the exit of Wawona Tunnel.

The famous and oft photographed Yosemite Waterfall generally dries up from the end of June to the start of the rains and snow in November. The other waterfalls, too, such as the Bridal Veil Falls, are only trickles during the summer months. About 2 miles (3 km) from the S entrance to the park lies Mariposa Grove, the Redwood grove that it is easiest to visit. There are two other Redwood groves, Tuolumne Grove and Merced Grove in the hinterland of the park. Visitors who have already been to Muir Woods (see entry) will see at once the difference between the two species of Redwood. In the latter grows the *Sequoia semper-*

129

virens which reaches a greater height but does not have so large a circumference as the *Sequoia giganteum* in the Yosemite Park. The *Sequoia giganteum* is among the world's largest plants.

In the grove at Mariposa there are about 500 of these immense trees. The largest, in the lower part of the grove, is called Giant Grizzly; it still stands some 220 ft (67 m) tall though its crown broke off under the weight of snow. The diameter at the base amounts to 30 ft (9 m), and some of its boughs which branch off at a height of 90 ft (27 m) are themselves 8 ft (2 m) in diameter. It is estimated that this tree is 2700 years old.

There are several hundred miles of footpaths through the park, and it is rewarding to explore them as far as time permits. It is important, however, to take sufficient supplies as there are no services of any kind outside the valley.

Not far from the Tioga road, the road into the park from the NE and open only in the summer months, there are several very beautiful mountain lakes. The finest is May Lake at an altitude of 7700 ft (2347 m). Equally worth while is an excursion to Glacier Point (7200 ft/2195 m) from which there are breathtaking views of the other peaks in the Yosemite Valley.

In Yosemite Village there are not only the hotels which have already been mentioned and which all have restaurants but also every sort of facility for shopping.

In the Visitors' Center all conceivable information about the park is available. It is here, too, that a permit must be obtained by visitors desiring to camp in the hinterland where there are 6 camp sites.

It has been accurately established that 76 species of mammals live in the park, among them the dangerous Grey Bear and the Brown Bear: respect the warning notices! There are also 221 species of birds, 29 species of reptiles, 37 species of trees and hundreds of different sorts of flowers and plants.

Zoo

See San Francisco Zoological Gardens

Practical Information

Airport

San Francisco International Airport is some 14 miles (22.5 km) S of downtown San Francisco.

Passengers can take taxis, Airporter buses or use the hotel limousine services.

Getting to downtown San Francisco

The fare is about $25 plus tip.

By taxi

Airporter buses connect the airport and the downtown Airline Terminal. The buses leave from in front of the airport's Central and South Terminals directly by the baggage checkout. From 6 a.m. to 10 p.m. they run every 15 minutes, from 10 p.m. to midnight every half hour and between midnight and 6 a.m. their times of departure depend on the incoming flights. It takes about 20 to 30 minutes to get from the airport, downtown to the Air Terminal, and costs $7.

By Airporter buses

The Air Terminal is located on the corner of Taylor Street and Ellis Street in the heart of the hotel district in the centre of San Francisco. For arrivals and departures of buses linking the airport and Air Terminal dial 673–2433.

Air Terminal

There are also limousines (mini-vans) which will take you direct to your hotel. Fare per person $9.

Limousines

Banks

Bank of America,
345 Montgomery Street, tel. 622–2451.
Mon.–Thurs. 9 a.m.–4 p.m.; Fri. until 6 p.m., Sat. until 1 p.m.

Bank of America,
Powell and Market Streets, tel. 622–4498.
Mon.–Thurs. 9 a.m.–4 p.m.; Fri. until 6 p.m., Sat. until 1 p.m.

Foreign Exchange Ltd.,
415 Stockton Street, tel. 397–4700.
Mon.–Fri. 8 a.m.–5.30 p.m., Sat. 9 a.m.–1.30 p.m.

Macy's California,
Stockton and O'Farrell Streets, 4th Floor, tel. 397–3333.
Mon.–Wed. 9.30 a.m.–8 p.m., Thurs. and Fri. until 9 p.m., Sat. until 6.30 p.m., Sun. 11 a.m.–6 p.m.

Thomas Cook,
100 Grant Avenue, tel. 362–3452.
Mon.–Fri. 9 a.m.–5 p.m.

Sandy beach in Aquatic Park

Beaches

Although San Francisco is almost totally surrounded by water it seldom gets warm enough to use the beaches for bathing. There is a small sandy beach in Aquatic Park but people tend to use this just for sunbathing and only a few hardy souls venture in for a swim because even in August the temperature of the water hardly ever exceeds 59°F (15°C).

For a swim in the ocean San Franciscans have to travel almost 70 miles (113 km) S to Santa Cruz and even there the season for bathing is a very short one.

Boat tours

Blue and Gold Fleet, tel. 781–7877, 1¼-hour tours on San Francisco Bay. Frequent departures from Pier 39 (West Marina) beginning at 10 a.m.

Hornblower Yachts, tel. 394–8900. Daily from Pier 33 at 7.30 p.m. (Sunday at 6 p.m.) a 3-hour dinner cruise; on Friday only at noon a 1½-hour lunch cruise; weekends at 11 a.m. a 2-hour "brunch" cruise in the bay, aboard the 164 ft (50 m) "City of San Francisco" which has three decks.

Red and White Fleet, tel. 546–2896. Frequent trips daily from Fisherman's Wharf (Piers 41 and 43½) from 10.45 a.m.; ¾-hour trips in the bay. Also trips to Sausalito, Tiburon, Alcatraz, Angel Island and Vallejo.

Bookshops

Books, Inc. & Tro Harper's,
140 Powell Street.
San Francisco's oldest bookshop, established in 1851.

City Lights,
261 Columbus Avenue.
Founded and run by the poet Lawrence Ferlinghetti
(see Famous People).

Dalton,
200 Kearny Street and 2 Embarcadero Center.

Doubleday,
265 Sutter Street.

International Corner,
500 Sutter Street.

Sierra Club,
730 Polk Street (Civic Center).

Waldenbrooks,
Embarcadero, Gallery at Crocker's, 941 Market Street and
129 Geary Street.

Breakdown patrol

If you have a breakdown in a rented car, inform the rental
company immediately (see Rent-a-car).
If your car is not rented call the California State Automobile
Association on 565–2012, or the American Automobile Association (AAA) national emergency number 1–800–336–HELP.
Visitors from abroad who bring in cars that are not made to US
standards should make sure they are in good working order
since the right spare parts will be very hard to come by,
although most big cities will have a dealer who can undertake
repairs to foreign cars.

Buses

See Railroads and buses, Public transportation.

Business hours

See Drugstores   Chemists

See Banks   Banks

Business hours are not subject to any laws, so shops and   Shops
restaurants can stay open as long as they please. There are
quite a few shops, supermarkets included, that open round the
clock right through the week.

Many shops in the main shopping centres on Union Square, Jackson Square and in Sutter Street close about 6.30 p.m. but some stay open until 9 p.m. or even longer. Macy's department store in Union Square is open from 8 a.m. to 10 p.m. Monday–Friday, Saturdays from 10 a.m. to 7 p.m. and Sundays from 11 a.m. to 6 p.m. A number of other shops have adopted the same hours and there are quite a few delicatessens, etc., that stay open until midnight or round the clock.
Almost all the shops in the shopping centres around Fisherman's Wharf (Ghirardelli Square, The Cannery, The Anchorage, Pier 39) stay open until 9 or 10 at night in the main season, at other times they close at 8.30 p.m.

Main shopping centres

See entries for particular museums in the A to Z section and the list headed "Museums" in Practical Information.

Museums

See Postal services

Post offices

Restaurants generally stay open until midnight or 1 a.m. Most of the eating places in the Zim chain are open round the clock.

Restaurants

Car hire

See Rent-a-car

Chemists

See Drugstores

Churches

Besides St Mary's Cathedral, Grace Cathedral, Old St Mary (see Chinatown entry) and the Mission Dolores which are described in the A to Z section, San Francisco has the following churches which warrant a mention:

First Baptist Church of San Francisco (1910), Market Street/Octavia Street.
First Unitarian Church (1889), 1187 Franklin Street.
Holy Trinity Russian Orthodox Cathedral (1909), 1520 Green Street.
Notre Dame des Victoires (cath., 1913), 566 Bush Street.
Old First Presbyterian (1911), Van Ness Avenue and Sacramento Street.
Russian Holy Virgin Cathedral of the Church in Exile (1961), 6210 Geary Boulevard.
St Boniface Church (cath., 1908), 133 Golden Gate Avenue.
St Francis of Assisi (cath., 1849), 610 Vallejo Street.
St Luke's Episcopal Church (1910), Van Ness Avenue and Clay Street.
St Mark's Evangelical Lutheran Church (1895), 1111 O'Farrell Street.
St Peter and St Paul Church (cath., 1924), 666 Filbert Street.
Trinity Episcopal Church (1892), 1668 Bush Street.

◀ *Cloudbanks over the Golden Gate Bridge*

Church of St Peter and St Paul

Synagogue

Temple Emanu-El (1927), Arguella Street/Lake Street.

Additional information

Only a handful of San Francisco's churches date from before the 1906 earthquake so that most of the city's churches built after that date are modelled on foreign lines.

Cinemas

See Movies

Consulates

United Kingdom: 9th floor Equitable Life Building,
                120 Montgomery Street, tel. 981–3030.
Canada: 1 Maritime Plaza 11th floor,
         Golden Gateway Center, tel. 981–2670.

Crime

General

San Francisco has its share of crime like any other big city. There are certain quarters that visitors should steer clear of or where they should be extremely careful. San Francisco is undoubtedly one of the most beautiful cities in the world, and by taking a few precautions it can also be made one of the safest.

Western Addition area which is bordered by Hayes Street (S), Geary Street (N), Gough Street (E) and Steiner Street (W) has recently been the scene of several tourist muggings so no one should walk through this area to get, say, from City Hall to Golden Gate Park, even though this may be the best route according to the map.

Do not try to take pictures of the Victorian houses with the Transamerica Pyramid (see A to Z) in the background from Alamo Square – the police patrol will tell you to move on anyway.

Currency

The basic US unit of currency is the dollar ($1.00) or 100 cents. Coins are minted in 1 cent (penny), 5 cents (nickel), 10 cents (dime), 25 cents (quarter), the less common 50 cents (half dollar) and one dollar. Paper money (referred to as bills) is printed in $1.00, $2.00, $5.00, $10.00, $20.00, $50.00 and $100.00 denominations. Notes of higher denominations are also available from banks within the US.

There are no restrictions on the amount of money visitors may bring in or take out of the United States. However, persons importing or exporting more than $10,000 in cash or monetary instruments will be required to state this on the customs declaration completed in the aircraft.

Foreign currency can be exchanged at San Francisco International Airport (see Airport) in the International Terminal (accessible by in- and out-bound passengers), at the following banks:

Bank of America – daily from 7 a.m. to 11 p.m.

Thomas Cook – daily from 7 a.m. to 11 p.m.

Since changing foreign currency in the USA is often difficult (no exchange in hotels; time-consuming checks at banks) and there is a generally a loss on the exchange rate, it is advisable to obtain US dollars in Europe before departure. For reasons of security visitors are recommended to purchase travellers' cheques (low rate of commision) from their own bank or from a European branch of American Express. Eurocheques are unsuitable for the USA. If your American Express cheques are lost or stolen they will usually be replaced by the nearest branch of the company on presentation of the sales advice note issued when the cheques were purchased.

It is advisable to have one of the major credit cards (American Express, Mastercard, Visa, Diner's Club, Carte Blanche), these often proving better than a passport as proof of identity. They can be used to settle a variety of "checks" (i.e. bills) in hotels, restaurants and shops, as well as for buying airline tickets. They also provide an accepted form of surety when renting a car.

Customs regulations

Articles for personal use (clothing, toilet articles, jewellery, photographic and film apparatus, binoculars, portable typewriters, portable radios, video and television apparatus, sports

equipment and even a car for 1 year) can be imported without payment of tax. In addition adults can bring in 1 quart (about 1 litre) of alcoholic drink, 300 cigarettes or 50 cigars or 3 lbs of tobacco. In addition every person can import presents up to a value of 100 US dollars including, for adults, up to 1 gallon (3·78 litres) of alcoholic drink and 100 cigars. There are special regulations for the import of live animals, meat, fruit and plants (information can be obtained from customs offices).

Department stores

See Shopping

Doctors

See Emergency calls

Drugstores

American drugstores, or pharmacies, are nothing like the regular European chemist's shop. For most of them dispensing prescriptions forms only a small part of their business and many of them are more like general stores where you can also get something to eat and drink.

For a list of chemists consult the "Drugstore" listing in the Yellow Pages ("Walgreen" is one of the city's best known). | Information

Usually 9 a.m. to 6 p.m.; some are open up until 9 p.m., possibly midnight. | Business hours

There is no organised night emergency service but it is always possible to make use of the nearest hospital (see Hospitals) since they all have their own pharmacies. | Emergency service

Electricity

110–115 volt, 60 cycle A.C. If you have an electric razor, hair-drier or iron that is not dual-voltage you require a voltage transformer (otherwise just an adapter plug) which you should bring with you. If you forget or lose your transformer or adapter, you can get one in a hardware store or a department store. (The hotel porter will be able to tell you where to go.)

Emergency calls

911 | Ambulance, Medical emergency, Fire Department, Police

◀ A last look at San Francisco with the yachts at Pier 39 in the foreground

Emergency Hospital   413–2800
                            821–8111

Events

Mid Jan.–early Mar.	Chinese New Year celebrations in Chinatown (Information: Chinese Chamber of Commerce, 730 Sacramento Street, tel. 982–3000.
End March/April	Easter Sunday Sunrise Festival, Mount Davidson.
Mid-April	Cherry Blossom Festival in the Japan Center, Post and Geary Streets: Japanese music, dancing, films, tea ceremony, Bonsai demonstrations, calligraphy, etc. (Information: tel. 922–6776.)
End April/May	International Film Festival (see movies).
May	Latin-American Fiesta and Parade (in Mission).
June	Cable Car Festival. Lesbian–Gay Parade.
4 July	On Independence Day Fireworks on the Crissy Field near the Marina.
August	Flower Show/Golden Gate Frestival, Golden Gate Park.
September	Japanese autumn festival (Aki Matsure) in the Japan Center. (Information: tel. 346–3242 or 922–6776.)
October	Columbus Day (Mon. before 12 October) Columbus Festival on the North Beach and on Fisherman's Wharf with grand procession.
End October/November	Rodeo, horse and cattle show in the Cow Palace, Geneva Avenue, tel. 469–6000.

Ferries

See Public transportation

Food and drink

Even if you lack the time or the money for a meal in a restaurant (see entry) you need never go hungry – there is almost always somewhere near by with fast food on offer.

Hamburger	A hamburger is a sandwich consisting of a patty of ground or chopped meat, seasoned with onions, cheese, etc., between two halves of a roll. The price ranges between 75 cents and $2.
Hot dogs	A hot dog is a frankfurter with mustard and sauerkraut, served in a split roll. Price about 80 cents.
Pizza pies	A pizza pie is an Italian-style pizza, with tomato sauce, pieces of sausage and cheese, which is eaten hot.

The most popular American form of sandwich is made of rye bread and corned beef, roast beef or pastrami eaten with a gherkin and a cup of coffee. Sandwiches are served in coffee shops, drugstores and at lunch counters.

Price categories

At breakfast and even at other meals the Americans drink lightly roasted and thin coffee or caffeine-free coffee ("sanka" or "postum"). A second cup of coffee, or tea (made with tea-bags) is often provided without further charge. Drinking chocolate and soft drinks, such as cola, tonic or fruit juice, sodas, club sodas (plain carbonated water) or milk and milk shakes can be obtained everywhere. These are often served "iced" unless otherwide ordered. Root beer, originally produced from the root and bark of the sassafras tree which, after fermentation, made a slightly alcoholic drink, can often be obtained in drugstores and from vending machines. Nowadays manufactured from water, sugar, a dark colouring agent and various spices, it is no longer alcoholic and at first taste not very pleasant.

Drinks

Beer is always served cold and is rather lighter than the beers found in Great Britain. It is served by the glass, stein, seidel, schooner or pitcher. Brands commonly encountered are Budweiser, Schlitz, Falstaff, Pabst, Busch, Lone Star, Coors, La Crosse and Miller as well as the popular and expensive imported beers (frequently from Germany).

Before a meal it is usual to have a cocktail, a mixed drink with a gin, vodka, vermouth or rum base, often given a fanciful name. Spirits (liquors) favoured by the Americans are: whiskey, (Bourbon, Scotch, Canadian, Rye, Irish or blended), vodka, gin, rum and brandy. In restaurants water, generally ice cold, is provided free with meals.

Galleries

Most of San Francisco's galleries are downtown in and around Sutter Street. Almost all have permanent exhibitions and most of them are open from 10 a.m. to 5 or 6 p.m. Monday to Saturday or Tuesday to Sunday. The following list gives some of the better known ones:

Allrich Gallery, 251 Post Street, tel. 398–8896.
Atelier Dore, inc., 771 Bush Street, tel. 391–2423.
Braunstein Gallery, 254 Sutter Street, tel. 392–5532.
Carlson Gallery, 257 Grant Avenue, tel. 982–2882.
Continental Art Gallery, 545 Sutter Street, tel. 982–7781.
Fraenkel Gallery, 55 Grant Avenue, tel. 981–2661.
Galerie DeTours, 701 Sutter Street, tel. 362–0504.
Gump's Gallery, 250 Post Street, tel. 982–1616.
Harcourts Gallery, 460 Bush Street, tel. 421–3428.
John Berggruen Gallery, 228 Grant Avenue, tel. 781–4629.
John Pence Gallery, 750 Post Street, tel. 441–1138.
Kertesz Fine Art Gallery, 521 Sutter Street, tel. 626–0376.
Laurence Ross Gallery, 377 Geary Street, tel. 434–3210.
Maxwell Galleries, 551 Sutter Street, tel. 421–5193.
Pasquale de Sarthe Gallery, 315 Sutter Street, tel. 397–0168.
Pasquale Iannetti Gallery, 522 Sutter Street, tel. 433–2771.
Richard Thompson Gallery, 80 Maiden Lane, tel. 956–2114.
Rorick Gallery, 643 Mason Street, tel. 885–1182.
San Francisco Art Exchange, 458 Geary Street, tel. 441–8840.
Vorpal Gallery, 393 Grove Street, tel. 397–2200.
Stephen Wirtz Gallery, 345 Sutter Street, tel. 433–6879.

Getting to San Francisco

Most of San Francisco's overseas visitors arrive by air, although the city is also a port of call for cruise liners. Scheduled international flights come into the International Terminal of San Francisco International Airport, some 14 miles (22.5 km) S of downtown San Francisco, while Oakland International Airport across the bay handles international charter flights.

Visitors arriving by air from abroad should bring at least $10 of small change with them in silver and dollar banknotes (bills) which they should keep handy for cab fares, telephone calls, tips, etc. (see entries), since getting change for banknotes of larger denominations can prove difficult (fear of forgeries).

Hotels

For its size San Francisco has more hotel rooms than any other comparable city, especially as in recent years many new luxury hotels have been built and this has brought the total number of rooms to nearly 40,000. This is usually enough to meet the demand, but when the city is hosting one or several conventions beds can be in short supply. In any case, if the visitor arrives in San Francisco in the evening a prior reservation is strongly recommended.

Breakfast is never included in the room charge and in fact many of the smaller hotels do not serve breakfast. Guests are under no obligation to have breakfast in their hotel and can always get what they want in a nearby diner, lunch counter, etc.

San Francisco's Hyatt Regency Hotel in Embarcadero Center

Entrance to the Mark Hopkins Hotel

Most hotels, especially the larger ones, have one or more restaurants with prices that vary according to the category of hotel.

All hotels have safes in which cash, jewellery or other valuables can be deposited. Room keys are not usually handed in to the desk clerks until checkout time (usually noon). Rooms can be paid for by travellers' cheques or by credit card (see Currency) and an additional tax, currently more than 11%, has to be added to the room charge.

There is no charge for children (individual hotels decide the age limit) occupying the same room as parents.

Almost all the hotels listed below have rooms with private bath, air conditioning and colour TV.

The hotels are listed alphabetically and divided into five price categories: **Price categories**

Luxury hotels (single room over $110, double room over $125).
High amenity hotels (single room $85–$90, double room $90– below $125).
Good quality hotels (single room $60–$75, double room $78– $90).
Reasonably priced hotels (single room $50–$60, double room $60–$75).
Very reasonably priced hotels (single room under $45, double room under $55).

Advance booking is strongly advisable. Any hotel with the dialling prefix 800 can be called up free of charge from any-where in the States (except Alaska and Hawaii).

143

Hotels

Luxury hotels

*Donatello (95 r.), 501 Post Street, tel. 441–7100/800–227–3184 (800–792–9837 within California).
*Fairmont Hotel and Tower (596 r.), 950 Mason Street, tel. 772–5000/800–527–4727.
*Four Seasons Clift (329 r.), 495 Geary Street, tel. 775–4700/800–332–3442.
*Grand Hyatt San Francisco (693 r.), 345 Stockton Street, tel. 398–1234/800–233–1234.
*Huntington (140 r.), 1075 California Street, tel. 474–5400/800–227–4683 (800–652–1539 within California).
*Hyatt Regency San Francisco (803 r.), 5 Embarcadero Center, tel. 788–1234/800–233–1234.
*Mark Hopkins Inter-Continental (391 r.), 1 Nob Hill, tel. 392–3434/800–327–0200.
*Meridien San Francisco, (675 r.), 50 Third Street, tel. 974–6400/800–543–4300.
*Nikko San Francisco, (525 r.), 222 Mason Street, tel. 394–1111/800-NIKKO-US.
*Pan Pacific Hotel San Francisco (330 r.), 500 Post Street, tel. 771–8600/800–553–6465.
*Parc Fifty Five (1003 r.), 55 Cyril Magnin Street, tel. 392–8000/800–338–1338.
*San Francisco Hilton on Hilton Square (1907 r.), 1 Hilton Square, tel. 771–1400/800–445–8667.
*San Francisco Marriott (1500 r.), 55 Fourth Street, tel. 896–1600/800–228–9290.
*Sheraton at Fisherman's Wharf (525 r.), 2500 Mason Street, tel. 362–5500/800–325–3535.
*Stouffer Stanford Court (402 r.), Nob Hill, tel. 989–3500/800–227–4736.
*Westin St Francis (1200 r.), Union Square, tel. 397–7000/800–228–3000.

High amenity hotels

Cathedral Hill (400 r.), 1101 Van Ness Avenue, tel. 776–8200/800–227–4730.
Clarion Hotel San Francisco Airport (435 r.), 401 East Millbrae Avenue, Millbrae, tel. 692–6363/800–CLARION.
Galleria Park (177 r.), 191 Sutter Street, tel. 781–3060/800–792–9639 (800-792-9855 in California).
Hilton at San Francisco International Airport, (529 r.), San Francisco International Airport, tel. 589–0770.
Holiday Inn – Financial District (566 r.), 750 Kearny Street, tel. 433–6600/800–HOLIDAY.
Holiday Inn – Fisherman's Wharf (580 r.), 1300 Columbus Avenue, tel. 771–9000/800–HOLIDAY.
Holiday Inn – Union Square (400 r.), 480 Sutter Street, tel. 398–8900/800–HOLIDAY.
Sheraton Palace (550 r.), 2 New Montgomery Street, tel. 392–8600/800–325–3535.
Sir Francis Drake (417 r.), 450 Powell Street, tel. 392–7755/800–227–5480 (800–652–1668 within California).

Good quality hotels

Bedford (144 r.), 761 Post Street, tel. 673–6040/800–227–5642 (800–652–1889 within California).
Bellevue (250 r.), 505 Geary Street, tel. 474–3600/800–421–8851.
Handlery Motor Inn (93 r.), 260 O'Farrell Street, tel. 986–2525/800–228–0838.
Holiday Inn – Civic Center (390 r.), 50 Eighth Street, tel. 626–6103/800–HOLIDAY.

Holiday Inn – Golden Gateway (500 r.), 1500 Van Ness Avenue, tel. 441–4000/800–HOLIDAY.

Howard Johnson's Motor Lodge (128 r.), 580 Beach Street, tel. 775–3800/800–654–2000 (800–652–1527 within California).

Miyako (218 r.), 1625 Post Street, tel. 922–3200/800–553–4567.

Ramada Hotel – Fisherman's Wharf (231 r.), 590 Bay Street, tel. 885–4700/800–228–2828.

Raphael (152 r.), 386 Geary Street, tel. 986–2000/800–821–5343.

Best Western Americania (142 r.), 121 Seventh Street, tel. 626–0200/800–444–5816.

Reasonably priced hotels

Best Western Canterbury Hotel/Whitehall Inn (275 r.), 750 Sutter Street, tel. 474–6464/800–227–4788 (800–652–1614 within California).

Best Western Civic Center Motor Inn (57 r.), 364 Ninth Street, tel. 621–2826/800–444–5829.

Best Western Grosvenor (206 r.), 380 South Airport Boulevard, tel. 873–3200/800–528–1234.

Best Western Miyako Inn (125 r.), 1800 Sutter Street, tel. 921–4000/800–528–1234.

Californian (243 r.), 405 Taylor Street, tel. 885–2500/800–227–3346 (800–622–0961 within California).

Handlery Union Square (378 r.), 351 Geary Street, tel. 781–7800/800–223–0888).

Holiday Lodge (75 r.), 1901 Van Ness Avenue, tel. 776–4469/800–367–8504.

King George (143 r.), 334 Mason Street, tel. 781–5050/800–288–6005.

Quality (132 r.), 2775 Van Ness Avenue, tel. 928–5000/800–221–2222.

Ramada Hotel San Francisco (460 r.), 1231 Market Street, tel. 626–8000/800–227–4747.

San Francisco Central Travelodge (84 r.), 1707 Market Street, tel. 621–6775/800–255–3050.

Savoy (83 r.), 580 Geary Street, tel. 441–2700/800–227–4223.

Vagabond Inn (132 r.), 2550 Van Ness Avenue, tel. 776–7500/800–522–1555 within California.

Villa Florence (177 r.), 225 Powell Street, tel. 397–7700/800–553–4411.

Beresford (114 r.), 635 Sutter Street, tel. 673–9900/800–533–6533.

Very reasonably priced hotels

Beresford Arms (102 r.), 701 Post Street, tel. 673–2600/800–533–6533.

Best Western El Rancho Inn (321 r.), 1100 El Camino Real, Millbrae, tel. 588–2912/800–826–5500.

Beverly Plaza (150 r.), 342 Grant Avenue, tel. 781–3566/800–227–3818.

Broadway Manor (60 r.), 2201 Van Ness Avenue, tel. 776–7900/800–727–6239.

Carlton (165 r.), 1075 Sutter Street, tel. 673–0242/800–227–4496 (800–792–0958 within California).

Cartwright (114 r.), 524 Sutter Street, tel. 421–2865/800–227–3844.

Chancellor (140 r.), 433 Powell Street, tel. 362–2004.

Commodore International (113 r.), 825 Sutter Street, tel. 923–6800/800–338–6848 (800–327–9157 within California).

Mark Twain (115 r.), 345 Taylor Street, tel. 673–2332/
800–227–4074 (800–622–0873 within California).
Pickwick (190 r.), 85 Fifth Street, tel. 421–7500/800–227–3282.
Prescott (167 r.), 545 Post Street, tel. 563–0303/800–283–7322.
Shannon Court (173 r.), 550 Geary Street, tel. 775–5000/800–
821–0493 (800–228–8830 within California).

Women's hotel | The Women's Hotel (14 r.), 642 Jones Street, tel. 775–1777.

Insurances

It is essential to take out short-term health and accident insurance when visiting the United States, since the costs of medical
treatment are high; and it is also advisable to have baggage
insurance and (particularly if you have booked a package holiday) cancellation insurance. Arrangements can be made
through your travel agent or insurance company; many companies running package holidays now include insurance as
part of the deal.

Within the United States foreign visitors can effect insurance
through the following companies:

American International Underwriters,
1225 Connecticut Avenue, NW, Suite 414,
Washington D.C. 20036.

Address in the UK:
120 Fenchurch Street,
London WC3M 5BP.

Jazz

See Nightlife

Language

British (and other) visitors may find it helpful to be reminded of
some of the differences between American and British usage.

British	American
autumn	fall
bill	check
billion – 1000 million (now widely accepted in Britain where traditionally a billion was a million million)	billion
biscuit	cracker, cookie
bonnet	hood (of car)
boot	trunk (of car)
braces	suspenders
caravan	trailer
carry-out	"to go" (in cafeteria, etc.)
cinema	movie (theater)
cloakroom	checkroom

cupboard	closet
dustbin	garbage can
first floor	second floor
flat	apartment
football	soccer
fortnight	two weeks
"gents" (lavatory)	men's room
graduation (university, etc.)	commencement
ground floor	first floor
handbag	purse
label	sticker
"ladies" (lavatory)	ladies' room, powder room
lavatory	rest room
lavatory (roadside)	comfort station
lift	elevator
lorry	truck
luggage	baggage
maize	corn
nappy	diaper
open square	plaza
pavement	sidewalk
personal call (on telephone)	person to person call
petrol	gas, gasoline
post	mail
post code	zip code
queue	(stand in) line
(railway) line, platform	track
refrigerator	icebox
return ticket	round trip ticket
reversed charge	collect (on telephone)
ring (up)	call (on telephone)
scone	biscuit
second floor	third floor
shop	store
single ticket	one-way ticket
spanner	wrench
subway	underpass
summer time	daylight saving time
surname	last name
tap	faucet
tin	can (e.g. of food)
tram	streetcar
trousers	pants
trunk call	long-distance call
underground	subway
viewpoint, viewing platform	observatory
Whitsun	Pentecost

It is perhaps worth a special reminder that in multi-storey buildings the Americans begin counting the storeys from street level, so that the American first floor is the British ground floor, the American second floor is the British first floor, and so on.

Lost and Found

BART Lost and Found Bureau
12th Street Station, City Center (Oakland), tel. 465–4100.
Open: Mon.–Fri. noon–6 p.m.

Movies

First-run movie-houses are now scattered throughout the city, although there is a concentration in the Marina District and Van Ness Avenue.

San Francisco Experience

The San Francisco Experience at Pier 39, 2nd level (tel. 982–7550), is a particularly interesting form of entertainment that is screened daily every half hour from 10 a.m. to 10 p.m. Using a host of projectors it realistically re-creates San Francisco and its history so that you can relive the '49 Gold Rush, the earthquakes of 1906 and 1989, the heyday of Flower Power and hippies in Haight-Ashbury, the Chinese New Year as celebrated in Chinatown and many other happenings.

Film festival

An important feature of San Francisco is its international Film Festival, usually held at the end of April and/or the beginning of May and the oldest of its kind in the States. Screenings take place at AMC Kabuki 8 Theaters, on Post and Fillmore Streets in Japantown, and other Bay Area locations (tel. 931–FILM for programme).
In recent years a number of top movie-makers have based themselves in San Francisco.

San Francisco in the movies

It is also worth pointing out that more movies have been set in San Francisco than in any other American city apart from New York, and its popularity with Hollywood is borne out by the long list of titles such as "Hello Frisco" (1924), "In Old San Francisco" (1927), "San Francisco Nights" (1928), "Frisco Jenny" (1933), "San Francisco" (1936), "San Francisco Docks" (1940), "Hello, Frisco, Hello" (1943), "Man from Frisco" (1944), "San Francisco Story" (1952), "Incident in San Francisco" (1971), "Slaughter in San Francisco" (1973).
And last but not least the TV series "The Streets of San Francisco".

Museums

Art museums

Asian Art Museum
See A to Z, Golden Gate Park

California Palace of the Legion of Honor
See A to Z, California Palace of the Legion of Honor

San Francisco Museum of Modern Art
See A to Z, Civic Center

M. H. de Young Memorial Museum
See A to Z, Golden Gate Park

Other museums

Believe it or not
See A to Z, Fisherman's Wharf

Cable Car Museum
See A to Z, Cable Cars

California Academy of Sciences
See A to Z, Golden Gate Park

California Historical Society
See A to Z, California Historical Society

California State Division of Mines Museum
See A to Z, Ferry Building

Chevron, A World of Oil
See A to Z, World of Oil, Chevron

Chinatown Wax Museum
See A to Z, Chinatown

Exploratorium
Palace of Fine Arts, 3601 Lyon Street, tel. 563–7337.
Open Wed. 10 a.m.–9.30 p.m.; Thurs.–Sun. 10 a.m.–
5 p.m. Closed Thanksgiving, Christmas Day, 4 July.
Technology and science

Haas-Lilienthal House
See A to Z, Haas-Lilienthal House

J. L. Magnus Memorial Museum
University of California
2911 Russell Street
Open Sun.–Fri. 10 a.m.–4 p.m.
Jewish customs

Mexican Museum
See A to Z, Mexican Museum

Mission Dolores
See A to Z, Mission Dolores

Museo Italo-Americano
Fort Mason, Building C, Marina Boulevard
tel. 673–2200
Open Wed.–Sun. noon–5 p.m.
Exhibits illustrating the art, culture and history of Italians who
have emigrated to the USA
Entry free

Musée Mécanique
in Cliff House, Great Highway
(at the western end of Sutro Heights Park)
Open daily 9 a.m.–4 p.m.
Mechanical musical instruments and toys

Museum of Money of the American West
See A to Z, Bank of California

National Maritime Museum
See A to Z, National Maritime Museum

Navy/Marine Corps/Coast Guard Museum
See A to Z, Navy/Marine Corps/Coast Guard Museum

Octagon House
See A to Z, Octagon House

Pioneer Hall
See A to Z, Pioneer Hall

J. D. Randall Junior Museum
199 Museum Way/Roosevelt Avenue
Open Mon.–Fri. 10 a.m.–5 p.m.
Children's zoo

San Francisco African-American Historical and Cultural Society
See A to Z, San Francisco African-American Historical and
Cultural Society.

San Francisco Craft and Folk Art Museum
Fort Mason, Building A, Marina Boulevard, tel. 775–0990
Open Tue.–Fri. and Sun. 11 a.m.–5 p.m.; Sat. 10 a.m.–5 p.m.
Temporary exhibitions on various themes of contemporary
society and popular art.
Entry free

San Francisco Fire Department Pioneer Memorial Museum
See A to Z, San Francisco Fire Department Pioneer Memorial
Museum

Society of California Pioneers
See A to Z, Pioneer Hall

Stanford University Museum of Art
See A to Z, Stanford University Museum of Art

Treasure Island Museum (Navy-Marine Corps-Coast Guard)
See A to Z, Navy-Marine Corps-Coast Guard Museum

University Art Museum
See A to Z, Berkeley

Wax Museum at Fisherman's Wharf
See A to Z Fisherman's Wharf

Wells Fargo History Museum
See A to Z, Wells Fargo History Museum

World Trade Center
See A to Z, Ferry Building

Music

General

San Francisco's rich musical life was greatly enhanced in the
fall of 1980 by the opening of the Louise M. Davies Symphony
Hall (see A to Z, Civic Center), which meant that the San Francisco Opera, the Symphony Orchestra and the San Francisco
Ballet no longer have to share the War Memorial Opera House.

San Francisco Opera

The San Francisco Opera was founded in 1923 and its director
from 1958 until 1981 was the Viennese conductor Kurt Herbert
Adler who, despite the shortness of the season (from early
September to early December), managed to bring it international fame by engaging singers of international reputation and
putting on a host of US first performances. From the summer of
1982 Terry McEwen, has been the director of the opera (Opera
House box office, tel. 864–3330).

San Francisco Symphony
Orchestra

Founded in 1911, the San Francisco Symphony Orchestra
moved into its own Louise M. Davies Hall (tel. 431–5400) in

September 1980 and under its present principal conductor, Herbert Blomstedt, gives concerts from September to the end of May.

This ballet company, which was formed in 1932, is the oldest of the permanent companies in the States where it has also made a good name for itself with its fine blend of traditional and modern choreography. The company's home is the War Memorial Opera House, the season extending from January to early May (enquiries, tel. 861–1177).

San Francisco Ballet

The Louise M. Davies Symphony Hall (see A to Z, Civic Center) is the main concert venue but some colleges of the San Francisco State University (tel. 469–2141), the San Francisco Conservatory of Music (564–8086) and Mills College in neighbouring Oakland also stage concerts. Concerts are also given by the Chamber Symphony of San Francisco (441–4636) and the San Francisco Sinfonia (922–3434). During the season there are also about 20 dance events per month in and around San Francisco.

Concerts

Programmes are published in the "San Francisco Examiner-Chronicle" weekend edition.

See Theatre

Theatre

Newspapers and periodicals

San Francisco has two main dailies:

Local papers

The "San Francisco Chronicle" (morning paper) comes out through the week, published from 925 Mission Street, tel. 777–1111.

The "San Francisco Examiner" (evening paper) also comes out through the week and is published from 110 Fifth Street, tel. 777–2424.

Both papers combine to bring out the weekend edition, the "San Franciso Examiner-Chronicle".

Other publications:
"San Francisco Progress" (Wed., Fri. and Sun.), published from 851 Howard Street, tel. 982–8022.

"San Francisco Bay Guardian Weekly" (Wed.), published from 2700 19th Street, tel. 824–7660.

There are also several papers in Chinese, French, German, Italian, Japanese, Korean, Portuguese, Russian, Spanish and Yiddish, only a few of them dailies.

Nightlife

Because the nightlife scene is constantly changing it is best to check in one of the dailies or to call up in advance, as some of the night spots do not have live entertainment through the week.

Jazz, Rock

Nightspots on Broadway (North Beach)

Club Mardi Gras, 1390 California Street, tel. 474–0332 (Reggae, Jazz).
Great American Music Hall, 859 O'Farrell Street, tel. 885–0750.
Hotel Utah, 500 Fourth Street, tel. 421–8308 (Rock).
Jazz Palace, 638 Broadway, tel. 434–0530 (Jazz and Blues).
Keystone Korner, 750 Vallejo Street, tel. 781–0697 (Jazz).
Kimball's, 300 Grove Street, tel. 861–5555 (Jazz).
Last Day Saloon, 406 Clement Street, tel. 387–6343 (Rock).
Mabuhay Gardens, 443 Broadway, tel. 956–3315 (Avant-garde Rock).
Pier 23 Café, Embarcadero, tel. 362–5125 (Dixieland Jazz).
Pier 39, Fisherman's Wharf.
Pier 47, Fisherman's Wharf, tel. 771–0377 (Jazz).
Plough and Stars, 116 Clement Street, tel. 751–1122 (Live Irish music).
Sound of Music, 162 Turk Street, tel. 885–9616 (Rock).
The Stone, 412 Broadway, tel. 391–8282 (Rock).
Wolfgang's, 901 Columbus Avenue, tel. 474–2995 (Jazz, Rock).

Discothèques

Buzzby's, 1436 Polk Street, tel. 474–4246.
Camelot, 3231 Fillmore Street, tel. 567–4004.
I Beam, 1748 Haight Street, tel. 668–6006.
Lehr's Cabaret Disco, 726 Sutter Street, tel. 673–1717.
Oasis, 11th and Folsom Streets, tel. 621–8119.
Palladium, 1031 Kearny Street, tel. 434–1308.
Rockin' Robin's, 1840 Haight Street, tel. 221–1960.
Trocadera Transfer, 520 Fourth Street at Bryant, tel. 495–6620.
VIS Club, 628 Divisadero Street, tel. 567–0660.

Passports and visas

See Travel documents

Postal services (US Mail)

The US Post Office is responsible only for American postal services (US Mail), including money transfer; telephone and telegram/cable services are operated by private corporations (see entries).

Letters within the United States: 25 cents for the first ounce, 21 cents for each additional ounce. Postcards 15 cents.
Airmail letters to Europe: 45 cents for each half ounce; post-cards: 36 cents; aerograms: 31 cents.
Stamps are best bought at a post office as there is a surcharge on stamps from hotel automats. An increase in both inland and overseas postage is probable.

General Post Office
7th and Market Streets
More convenient post offices are located in the basement of Macy's department store on Union Square and at 130 Sutter Street.
Open: Mon.–Fri. 9.30 a.m.–5.30 p.m., Sat. 9.30 a.m.–1 p.m.

Usually Mon.–Fri. 8.30 a.m.–6 p.m., Sat. 9 a.m.–noon. The General Post Office is open round the clock.
Outside business hours stamps are obtainable from coin automats.

Poste restante mail should be marked "General Delivery".

The zip code is a five-figure post code following the two letter abbreviation for the state: e.g. San Francisco, CA 94100.

Mailboxes are letter-boxes painted blue with "US Mail" on them in white.

See Telephone and telegrams.

Postal rates · *General Post Office* · *Business hours* · *Telephone and telegrams*

Programme of events

The programme for the current week is published in the "San Francisco Examiner-Chronicle", printed at weekends.

Public holidays

Like the whole of the United States of America, San Francisco observes relatively few public holidays and even on these – with the exception of Easter Sunday, Christmas and New Year – many businesses remain open. However, banks, the Stock Exchange, administrative offices and schools are closed.
There is no extra public holiday at Christmas or Easter. Whitsun is not recognised.

Public transportation

The dates of the majority of official public holidays are fixed annually and, in order to extend weekends, are often transferred to a Monday before or after the actual holiday.

Statutory public holidays

New Year's Day (1 January), Martin Luther King Day (3rd Monday of January), Lincoln's Birthday (12 February), Washington's Birthday (Monday before 22 February), Easter Sunday, Memorial Day (30 May or last Monday of May), Independence Day (4 July), Labor Day (1st Monday of September), Columbus Day (12 October or 2nd Monday of October), Veterans' Day (11 November, commemorating the end of the First World War), Thanksgiving Day (4th Thursday of November), Christmas Day (25 December).

Public transportation (No Smoking on local services)

Buses, trams, metro

Cable car

The network of bus routes operated by MUNI, San Francisco Municipal Railway, is the most important means of transport of the inner city. There is a 24hr service on some routes. The basic fare is at present 85 cents (seniors 15 cents) – exact change required, with the facility of two changes of route within 90 minutes. The trams running only on Sundays in Market Street and the MUNI-Metro which runs on weekdays, can also be used with a transfer ticket.

The fare on the cable cars is $2, the ticket being valid for a period of two hours. Tickets are only available from self-service ticket machines at terminals and all major stops.

Signs for San Francisco's public transport: MUNI and BART

You can buy a one-day, or three-day, "Passport" ticket valid for all MUNI vehicles (including cable cars). The three-day ticket costs $10, one-day $6. They are available from MUNI at 949 Presidio Avenue, the San Francisco Visitor Center, City Hall, Cable Car Museum, and the Victorian Park turnaround (Fisherman's Wharf). The one-day ticket can also be obtained from cable car ticket machines (see above). Tickets also provide admission discounts at major museums, theatres and attractions.

There is a full map of the bus routes in the Yellow Pages which can be found in almost every hotel room.

For further information, call Municipal Railway Information Bureau, 673–MUNI.

BART stands for Bay Area Rapid Transit, the subway and surface rail system that since 1974 links San Francisco with communities on the E side of San Francisco Bay – N to Richmond, E to Concord (the most scenic and interesting route) and S to Fremont.

BART has 34 stations, eight of them in San Francisco. These are: Main and Market, Montgomery and Market, Powell and Market, 8th Street and Market, 16th Street and Mission, Bosworth and San José, Geneva and San José and Daly City. They operate 4 a.m. to midnight (Saturday from 6 a.m. to midnight, Sunday from 8 a.m. to midnight).

The fare depends on the length of the journey and ranges between 75 cents and $2.
The ticket automats near the turnstiles take nickels, dimes and quarters (5, 10 and 25 cents) as well as $1.00 and $5.00 banknotes and give change.
After you feed your ticket into the slot near the turnstiles, it will be returned to you with a code.
When leaving the station at your destination you have to feed the ticket back into the slot again. If you have overpaid it will be returned and the balance can go towards the next ride. If you have underpaid the sign "Underpaid Go To Adfare" will light up and the Adfare machine will tell you how much more you have to pay.

Visitors can buy an excursion ticket for $2.60 and ride anywhere throughout the 71 mile (114 km) system. No additional fare is required so long as the traveller does not exit at a station en route and the traveller must return to the station where the trip began.

For information call 788–BART at any time.

The BART lost and found is in the station at 12th Street and City Center in Oakland and is open noon to 6 p.m. Monday to Friday, tel. 465–4100.

Before the bridges spanning the bay and the BART line were built, the ferries were the most important link between San Francisco on one side of the bay and Marin Country, Oakland and the communities on the other. Nowadays they have completely lost their importance.

Ferry boat services still depart several times a day to Sausalito and Larkspur from, facing the Bay, the right-hand side of the Ferry Building (see A to Z) and from the left-hand side to Tiburon and Vallejo.

During the summer and on holidays and weekends a ferry service operates from Pier 43½ at Fisherman's Wharf to Tiburon and Angel Island.

From Pier 41 there is a year-round ferry to Alcatraz and Vallejo.

For exact departure times call the following numbers:
332–6600 for Sausalito and Larkspur.
546–BOAT for Tiburon, Angel Island, Alcatraz and Vallejo.

Radio, TV

Radio

Radio stations rarely transmit live programmes. Most of them rely on tapes and records. There are some radio channels that specialise in classical, jazz and rock music while others focus on particular ethnic groups. Other channels send out news bulletins all day long. (Hertz frequency.)

KCBS (740) news only
KSFO (560)
KFRC (610) mainly rock music
KNBR (680)
KGO (810) news and live current events programmes
KNEW (910) mainly country music
KABL (960) light music
KIOI (1010)
KKHI (1550) classical music
KEST (1450) religious, foreign language and live current events programmes

TV

The daily programme for the eight TV channels is published in the dailies and the programme for the week is given in the weekend editions (see Newspapers and periodicals).

The major channels are:
4 KRON, NBC
5 KPIX, CBS/Westinghouse Broadcasting
7 KGO ABC
9 KOED, PBS (Public Broadcasting, no commercials)
2 KTVU, Cox Broadcasting (from Oakland)
11 KNTV, ABS (from San José)
14 KBHK, Fields Communications Corporation
20 KEMO, Crosby Productions

Railroads and buses

Southern Pacific Railroad

Since the railways (railroad) plays a relatively small part in US long-distance transportation nowadays, visitors to San Francisco are unlikely to travel by train unless they use the commuter rail service to the suburbs operated by the Southern Pacific Railroad, which used to be the most important of the private railways serving the city. The Southern Pacific Railroad depot in San Francisco is at 4th and Townsend Streets (tel. 495–4546).

AMTRAK

What is left of long-distance rail traffic (trains to Los Angeles, the Midwest and the North) departs not from San Francisco but from the Amtrak Station at 16th and Wood Streets in Oakland which is the terminal for Amtrak, America's National Railroad and Passenger Corporation.

Shuttle buses operated by Amtrak transport passengers (who must have an Amtrak ticket valid to or from San Francisco) between the Oakland depot and San Francisco's Transbay Terminal at 1st and Mission Streets (tel. 800–USA RAIL). The buses depart from the Transbay Terminal about half an hour prior to a scheduled train departure from Oakland.

Amtrak, which covers approximately 26,000 miles of track and serves 500 cities and towns, also operates special fare schemes such as the USA Rail Pass which can only be purchased outside the USA and is valid for unlimited coach class travel within the selected period of validity between all points of the Amtrak system.

The Amtrak appointed agents in the UK are:

Albany Travel, 190 Deansgate, Manchester, tel. (061) 833 0202.
Compass, 9 Grosvenor Gardens, London SW1H 0BH, tel. (071) 828 4111.
Destination Marketing, York Road, London SW11 3TW, tel. (071) 978 5212.
Thistle Air, Bank Street, Kilmarnock, Ayrshire, tel. (0563) 71159.

State-of-the-art trains provide a daily service between San Francisco and San José. Trains leave from the terminal at Fourth and Townsend Streets (tel. 800–558–8661 within Northern California). Shuttle buses transport passengers to the Amtrak depot in Oakland.

CalTrain

Buses are considerably more important than railroads for both local and long distance transportation.

Buses

Local services:
Samtrans (southbound)
from Transbay Terminal
First and Mission Streets, tel. 761–7000/800-660-4BUS;
AC Transit (eastbound)
from Transbay Terminal
First and Mission Streets, tel. 839–2882;
Golden Gate Transit (to Marin and Sonoma counties) from Transbay Terminal
First and Mission Streets, tel. 332–6600

Long distance services:
Greyhound
from 7th and Mission Street, tel. 433–1500;
Trailways
Transbay Terminal
Mission and 1st Street, tel. 982–6400

UK addresses:
Greyhound International, 14/16 Cockspur Street, London SW1, tel. (071) 839 5591;
Trailways, Balfour House, 590 Uxbridge Road, Hayes, Middlesex UB4 0RY, tel. (081) 561 4656.

Reduced fares
The bus companies standardly offer special reductions (e.g. the

"See America" bus pass) allowing unlimited travel throughout the USA for a specific period. This is considerably less expensive than buying tickets for each individual journey.

Rent-a-car

There is really no need to rent a car to visit downtown San Francisco. Most visits can be made on foot and driving in a city with 43 hills can be pretty difficult, particularly when it comes to trying to park on the steep slopes of the streets where the native San Franciscan is at a definite advantage over the visitor. The clinching factor is the excellence of the public transportation system which will get you to almost any point in San Francisco, even if this means the occasional transfer. If you do have to get somewhere in a hurry there are plenty of cruising taxis – free if the rooflight is lit up – that can be hailed from the pavement. It is worth renting a car for excursions outside the city, down to Southern California or to other parts of the United States.

Documents

You must be able to produce a valid driving licence: British licences and those of certain other countries are acceptable. Payment should be made by an internationally recognised credit card (American Express, Mastercard or Visa) since cash customers may be asked to make large cash deposits.
Cars can be rented and picked up from the following firms which almost all have offices at the airport and in downtown San Francisco:
The first telephone number given below is that of the taxi firm's city office, the second is that of the airport and the third (where

Parking made difficult on the slopes of San Francisco

given) is the free 800 number which can be called from any-
where within the United States.

Alamo, 656 Geary Street, tel. 771–9717; 347–9911; 800–327–
9633.

Avis, 675 Post Street, tel. 885–5011; 877–6780; 800–331–1212.

Budget, 321 Mason Street, tel. 875–6850; 877–4477; 800–527–
0700.

Dollar, 333 Taylor Street, tel. 673–2137; 952–6200; 800–800–
4000.

Hertz, 433 Mason Street, tel. 771–2200; 877–1600; 800–654–
3131.

Payless, 415 Taylor Street, tel. 771–7711; 872–6565.

Thrifty, 290 Washington Street, tel. 673–6675; 692–0660;
800–367–2277.

Be sure to call up more than one car rental firm and compare
rates. Local firms often offer budget rates especially for week-
long rentals. Some firms charge for mileage on top of the basic
rental while others give you a certain amount of free mileage
and you can be charged for dropping off the car elsewhere than
in San Francisco.

Additional information

Restaurants

San Francisco has an incredible number of restaurants (of
which some 1800 are listed in the Yellow Pages alone) and an
astonishing variety of national cuisines.

General

Besides Chinese, Japanese, French, Italian and seafood restaurants and eating places with a typically American menu San
Francisco also offers an opportunity to get acquainted with
Moroccan, Brazilian, Peruvian, Vietnamese, Korean, and many
other foreign dishes.

San Francisco is particularly famous for its many seafood restaurants where besides all kinds of other fish, shellfish and
crustaceans, visitors can sample one of the many dishes
prepared from abalone (a kind of edible mollusc), the local
delicacy.

A restaurant meal is also an ideal opportunity to try the excellent Californian red and white wines.

There are restaurants over a wide price range. In Chinatown
(where you will also find some Japanese restaurants in the
vicinity) you can eat well and relatively cheaply. Almost all
restaurants accept credit cards (American Express, Mastercard, Visa and sometimes Diner's Club and Carte Blanche).
Table booking is advisable particularly in more expensive restaurants and at weekends.

See Business hours

Opening times

The type of cooking is indicated after the name of the restaurant.

A   =American
Ar =Armenian
C   =Chinese
Ca =Californian
Co =Continental
F   =French
G   =German

Restaurants

Gr =Greek
H =Hawaiian
Hu =Hungarian
I   =Italian
In =Indian
Int =International
J   =Japanese
M =Mexican
Mo=Moroccan
P   =Polynesian
R   =Russian
SF =Seafood
Sp =Spanish
St =Steak
Sw=Swiss

Chinatown

Cathay House (C), 718 California Street, tel. 982–3388.
Empress of China (C), 838 Grant Avenue, tel. 434–1345.
Four Seas (C), Grant Avenue, tel. 397–5577.
Imperial Palace (C), 919 Grant Avenue, tel. 982–4440.
Kan's (C), 708 Grant Avenue, tel. 982–2388.
Kinokawa (J), 347 Grant Street, tel. 956–6085.
Ryumon (C), 646 Washington Street, tel. 421–3868.
Yamato (J), 717 California Street, tel. 397–3456.

Downtown

Bardelli's (I), 243 O'Farrell Street, tel. 982–0243.
Brasserie Chambord (F), 152 Kearny Street, tel. 434–3688.
Caravansery (Ar), 310 Sutter Street, tel. 362–4640.
Donatello (I), 501 Post Street, tel. 441–7182 (expensive).
Fleur de Lys (F), 777 Sutter Street, tel. 673–7779 (expensive).
Iron Horse (I), 19 Maiden Lane, tel. 362–8133.
La Mère Duquesne (F), 101 Shannon Alley, tel. 776–7600.
Le Central (F), 453 Bush Street, tel. 391–2233.
"Lefty" O'Doul's (A), 333 Geary Street, tel. 982–8900.
Lehr's Greenhouse (H), 740 Sutter Street, tel. 474–6478.
Le Trianon (F), 242 O'Farrell Street, tel. 982–9353 (expensive).
Little Omar's Café (Ar), 208 Powell Street, tel. 781–1010.
The Magic Pan (Co), 341 Sutter Street, tel. 788–7397.
Marrakech (Mo), 419 O'Farrell Street, tel. 776–6717.
Masa's (F), 648 Bush Street, tel. 989–7154 (very expensive).
Omar Khayyam's (Ar), 196 O'Farrell Street, tel. 781–1010.
Salmagundi (souperie), 442 Geary Street, tel. 441–0894 (self-service).
Sam's Grill (SF), 374 Bush Street, tel. 421–0594.
Tadich Grill (SF), 240 California Street, tel. 391–2373.
Trader Vic's (Int), 20 Cosmo Place, tel. 776–2232 (expensive).

Hotel restaurants in Downtown:
Four Seasons – Clift Hotel, 495 Geary Street
   French Room (F), tel. 775–4700 (expensive).
Grand Hyatt San Francisco, 345 Stockton Street
   Hugo's One Up (Co), on the 36th floor, tel. 398–1234 (expensive).
   The Plaza (Ca), tel. 398–1234.
San Francisco Hilton on Hilton Square, 1 Hilton Square
   Chef's Table (Co), tel. 771–1400 (expensive).
   Henri's Room at the Top (Co), on the 46th floor, tel. 771–1400.

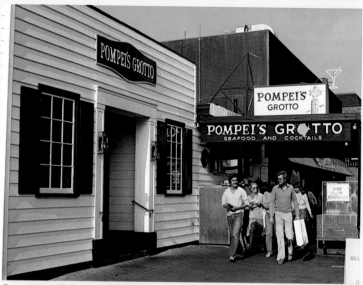

Restaurant at Fisherman's Wharf

Sir Francis Drake Hotel, 450 Powell Street
  Drake's Tavern (Co), tel. 392–7755.
  Carving Board (Co), tel. 392–7755.
  Starlite Roof (Co), tel. 392–7755 (lunch only, dancing in
  the evenings).
Westin St Francis Hotel, Union Square
  English Grill (SF), tel. 774-0233
  Victor's (Ca), tel. 956-7777 (expensive).

Carnelian Room (A), 555 California Street, tel. 433–7500   Financial district
(expensive).
Enzo's Ristorante (I), 3 Embarcadero Center, tel. 981–5530.
Ernie's (F), 847 Montgomery Street, tel. 397–5969 (expensive).
Jack's (F), 615 Sacramento Street, tel. 986–9854.
Lafayette (SF), 290 Pacific Avenue, tel. 986–3366.
Schroeder's (G), 240 Front Street, tel. 421–4778.

Hotel restaurants in the Financial District:
Hyatt Regency San Francisco, 5 Embarcadero Center
  Hugo's (Co), tel. 788–1234 (expensive).
  Equinox (A), on the 18th floor, tel. 788–1234.
  Market Place (A), tel. 788–1234.

Franciscan (SF), Pier 43½, tel. 362–7733.   Fisherman's Wharf
Lolli's Castagnola's (SF), 286 Jefferson Street, tel. 776–5015.
Pompei's Grotto (SF), 340 Jefferson Street, tel. 776–9265.
Scoma's (SF), Pier 47, tel. 771–4383.
Tarantino's (SF), 206 Jefferson Street, tel. 775–5600.

Shopping

Hotel restaurants in Fisherman's Wharf:
Sheraton at Fisherman's Wharf, 2500 Mason Street
Grand Exhibition (A), tel. 982–5536 (expensive).

Ghirardelli Square

Gaylord (In), 900 North Point, tel. 771–8822.
Lanzone & Son (I), 900 North Point, tel. 771–2880.
Mandarin (C), 900 North Point, tel. 673–8812.
Paprikas Fono (Hu), 900 North Point, tel. 441–1223.

North Beach

Beethoven (G), 1701 Powell Street, tel. 391–4488.
Greek Taverna (Gr), 256 Columbus Avenue, tel. 362–7260.

Nob Hill

Alexis (F), 1001 California Street, tel. 885–6400 (expensive).
Big Four (Co), Huntington Hotel, 1075 California Street, tel. 771–1140 (expensive).
Fournou's Ovens (Co), 905 California Street, tel. 989–1910 (expensive).

Hotel restaurants on Nob Hill:
Fairmont Hotel and Tower, 950 Mason Street
Venetian Room (Co), tel. 772–5163 (expensive).
Tonga Room (C), tel. 772–5278.
The Squire Restaurant (FCo), tel. 772–5211 (expensive).
Crown Room (buffet), on the 29th floor, tel. 772–5131.
Brasserie (A/Co), tel. 772–5199 (open 24 hours).

Pier 39

Chic's Place (SF), Pier 39, tel. 421–2442.
Dante's Sea Catch (SF), Pier 39, tel. 421–5778.
Neptune's Palace (SF), Pier 39, tel. 434–2260.

Telegraph Hill

Julius' Castle (Co), 1541 Montgomery Street, tel. 362–3042 (expensive).

Fort Mason

Green's at Fort Mason (Building A), tel. 771–6222 is San Francisco's most interesting vegetarian restaurant, run by the San Francisco Zen Center.

Shopping

Department stores

San Francisco does not have a great many department stores apart from:
Emporium, 853 Market Street, tel. 764–2222
Gump's, 250 Post Street, tel. 982–1616
I, Magnin, Union Square, tel. 362–2100
Macy's, Union Square, tel. 397–3333
Neiman-Marcus, 150 Stockton Street, tel. 362–3900
Nordstrom, San Francisco Shopping Center, tel. 243–8500
Saks Fifth Avenue, 384 Post Street, tel. 986–4300

Business hours

Most department stores open for business between 8.30 and 10 a.m. The smaller stores close around 5.30 p.m.; most of the larger ones stay open until 8 p.m. three or five days a week, and are open on Sundays.

Shopping centres

San Francisco's main shopping centres are around Union Square, including the $140 million, nine-storey, San Francisco Shopping Center opened in 1988, and the Crocker Galleria, modelled after Milan's Galleria Vittorio Emmanuelle. Other areas are around Jackson Square, in Cow Hollow, Chinatown, and the Embarcadero Center (see entries in A to Z), plus the various Fisherman's Wharf shopping and restaurant complexes (Ghirardelli Square, The Anchorage, The Cannery, and Pier 39).

Speciality shops

Lack of space means there is only room in this guide to mention a few of the many shops, mostly situated downtown, in San Francisco.

See Bookshops

Bookshops

Hoogasian, 250 Post Street (at Gump's), 480 Sutter Street and 1674 Lombard Street.
Podesta Baldocchi, 2525 California Street.
There are many flower stalls around Union Square, on Market Street, etc.

Flowers

Sour-dough bread is a local speciality which has been baked in the city since its early days when the recipe was brought here by an immigrant baker from France in 1849. The Boudin bakery

Bread

A great variety of flower shops and stalls

Sour Dough – a San Francisco speciality

and shops which are still owned by the family are on Fisher-man's Wharf (see A to Z) but sour-dough bread is on sale in almost every shop in San Francisco and at the airport.

Camera shops	AA International Cameras Electronics, 206 Powell Street. Brooks Cameras, 45 Kearny Street. Camera Boutique, 250 Kearny Street. Discount Camera Video, 624 Pine Street.
Souvenirs	Cost Plus, 2552 Taylor Street (Fisherman's Wharf). The Mole Hole, 1895 Union Street. The Penthouse Galleria, 325 Bush Street. Takahashi, 59 Grant Avenue and Mustard Building, Ghirardelli Square.
Women's fashions	L. M. Alcotts, 1799 Union Street. Courrèges, 155 Maiden Lane. Jessica McClintock, 353 Sutter Street. Helga Howie, 140 Maiden Lane. Lanz, 152 Maiden Lane. I. Magnin, Geary and Stockton Streets (Union Square). The Town Squire, 1318 Polk Street. Victoria's Secret, 395 Sutter Street.
General clothing	Brook Brothers, 201 Post Street. Bucks, 2351 Market Street, near Castro Street. Cassidy, 969 Market Street. Neiman-Marcus, 150 Stockton Street. Saks Fifth Avenue, 384 Post Street.
Men's clothing	Ariston, 349 Sutter Street. Livingston's, 100 Post Street.

Lion's Den, 822 Mission Street.
Rochester Big and Tall Clothing, Mission and Third Streets.
Wilkes Bashford, 336 Sutter Street.

Antoinette's, 276 Post Street.   Jewellery
Boring and Company, 140 Geary Street.
Harry Fireside, 219 Sutter Street.
Gold and More, 402 Sutter Street.
Pearl Empire, 127 Geary Street.
Tiffany's, 252 Grant Avenue.

See Business hours   Opening times

Sightseeing tours

A great number of organised sightseeing tours can be made by
bus, boat, helicopter and on foot. Brochures are available in the
hotels where bookings can be made. It is advisable to book a
day in advance, except for boat tours (with the exception of the
trip to Alcatraz).

Since San Francisco is particularly suited for exploration on   Walking tours
foot, there are a great number of tours, some of which do not
take place every day.

City Guides, tel. 557–4266 for recorded schedule.
Free city tours organised by the Friends of the San Francisco
Public Library (from where you can pick up a printed schedule).
Tours last approximately 1½ hours and run throughout the
week.

San Francisco Discovery Tours, tel. 673–2894.
Walks in the less well known parts of the city. Information from
the above telephone number.

JJ Walking Tours, tel. 567–7494.
Morning and afternoon 2-hour strolls through San Francisco,
daily at 10.30 a.m. and 2.30 p.m.; assemble at Cameron House,
920 Sacramento Street.
Evening tour of Chinatown at 6.15; assemble at Chinese Six
Companies Center, 843 Stockton Street.

Friends of Recreation and Parks, tel. 221–1311.
Offer free guided walking tours of the Golden Gate Park at
weekends from May to October, departing at 11 a.m. and 2 p.m.
(tours last 1½ to 2 hours). For assembly points call the above
number.

Heritage Walks, tel. 441–3004.
Tours organised by the Foundation for San Francisco's Architectural Heritage emphasising the city's history, and cultural
institutions in the Pacific Heights district, also Chinatown and
the Presidio on Saturdays in summer.

Street Walkers of San Francisco, tel. 392–5660.
All-day tours which combine walking with some use of cable
cars and buses, and including lunch in a Chinatown restaurant.

Sightseeing tours

Chinatown Discovery Tours, tel. 982–8839.
A tour offering an insight into Chinatown seldom seen by the visitor who doesn't venture off Grant Avenue. Tour is available with or without a Dim-Sum lunch, or dinner. Call for schedule.

Chinese Culture Center, tel. 986–1822.
For groups (six or more) only by prior arrangement. A walk through Chinatown with a Dim-Sum lunch.
For individuals and groups by prior arrangement, on Wednesdays at 10.30 a.m. A Walk through Chinatown. Tours leave from the Chinese Culture Center, 750 Kearny Street, on the second floor of the Holiday Inn.

Car tours

49 Mile Scenic Drive.
This 49 mile (79 km) sightseeing drive round the city, starting from the Civic Center (see A to Z) is signposted by blue and white seagull signs and takes in practically all San Francisco's major points of interest (allow at least three hours).

Bus tours

Dolphin Tours, tel. 441–6810.
Daily: a 7-hour tour at 10 a.m., half-day tours at 10 a.m. and 1.30 p.m. Also half-day tours at the same times to Muir Woods and Sausalito. A 9-hour tour daily to the Napa and Sonoma Valleys, Pick up at your hotel.

Golden City Tours, tel. 692–3044.
City tours twice daily. Pick up from your hotel between 8.30 and 9 a.m. and between 3 and 3.30 p.m. Also a city tour lasting 6 hours and a 7-hour tour to the vine-growing district (Napa and Sonoma).

Golden Gate Tours, tel. 788–5775.
Daily: 3½ hour tour of the city at 9.30 a.m. (also at 2 p.m. in summer); 3½-hour to Muir Woods and Sausalito, at 2 p.m. (also at 9.30 a.m. in summer). Whole-day tour to Monterey and Carmel on Tuesdays, Thursdays and Sundays at 9.30 a.m. Whole-day tour to the vine-growing district – for groups daily at 9.30 a.m. and for individuals at 9 a.m. Pick up from your hotel.

Gray Line, tel. 558–9400.
Five (six in summer) 3½-hour tours daily, first one at 9 a.m.; city tours combined with a boat trip at 9 a.m.,10 a.m. and 11 a.m.; two San Francisco by night tours daily at 7 p.m. (including a meal in Chinatown) and 8 p.m. plus many more. All tours leave from the Gray Line Terminal at 1st and Mission Streets.

Great Pacific Tour Company, tel. 626–4499.
Daily 3½-hour tours of the city at 9 a.m., 11 a.m. and 2 p.m., and to Muir Woods and Sausalito at 9 a.m. and 1.30 p.m. Also full-day tours to Monterey and Carmel (daily May to October; Wednesday to Sunday rest of year), and to the Sonoma and Napa wine country (daily May to October; Tuesdays, Thursdays and Saturdays the rest of the year).

Boat tours

See Boat tours

Helicopter tours

Commodore Helicopter Tours, tel. 332–4482.
Operates daily 9.30 a.m. to sunset from Pier 43, Fisherman's Wharf; 4-minute flights over the bay at a height of 650 ft (198 m).

Boat and helicopter tours take place weather permitting; if in doubt about the weather conditions, contact the firms concerned.

All the bus companies that operate city tours also provide day-long trips outside San Francisco. These include: Sausalito, Muir Woods and bay trip – Dolphin, Golden Gate, Gray and Great Pacific.
Sonoma and the Napa Valley wine country – City, Gray and Great Pacific.
Monterey, 17 Mile Drive and Carmel – Golden Gate, Gray and Great Pacific.
Yosemite National Park – Gray (daily 7 a.m.).

In the surrounding countryside

There are also flights to Yosemite operated by Yosemite Air San Francisco, tel. 931–2544.

Sports

San Francisco Giants, from April to the end of September, Candlestick Park on Bayshore Freeway 8 miles (13 km) S of San Francisco, for information call 467–8000 or 982–9400.
Oakland Athletics, April to the end of September in Oakland Coliseum (Information: tel. 638–0500).

Baseball

San Francisco 49ers, Sundays from August to December, Candlestick Park some 8 miles (13 km) S of San Francisco on Bayshore Freeway (information tel. (408) 562–4949).

Football

San Francisco has four public golf courses:
Harding Park Course, Skyline and Harding Park Boulevard, tel. 664–4690 or 661–1865.
Lincoln Park Course, 34th Avenue and Clement Street, tel. 221–9911.
Golden Gate Park Course, 47th Avenue and Fulton Street, tel. 751–8987.
Sharp Park Course, Highway 1 in Pacifica, tel. 359–3380.

Golf

Bay Meadows Racecourse in San Mateo, at the intersection of US 101 and Highway 92 (20 miles/32 km S of San Francisco), tel. 574–7223. Racing from August to January, daily except Mondays and Tuesdays.

Racing

Golden Gate Park Stables, Golden Gate Park, Kennedy Drive and 36th Avenue, tel. 668–7360.

Horseback riding

San Francisco has over 100 public tennis courts, all free of charge apart from the 21 courts in Golden Gate Park; for information and booking call up 753–7101.

Tennis

San Francisco Tennis Club, a private club at 645 Fifth Street (tel. 777–9000), has 12 indoor and 16 outdoor courts open to visitors on payment.

Stations

See Railroads and buses, Public transportation

Taxis (Cabs)

The minimum fare for the first mile (1·6 km) is $2.90 plus $1.50 for each additional mile. Waiting time is 20 cents a minute. Since there are no great distances in San Francisco, apart from the parts of the city near the sea, a taxi ride is usually relatively inexpensive.

The trip between downtown San Francisco and the airport costs about $25.
San Francisco has plenty of taxis and they can be picked up in the street.

The following firms generally operate a 24-hour service:
Checker Cab   626–2345
City Cab   468–7212
Classic Cab   584–2756
De Soto Cab   673–1414
Luxor Cab   282–4141
Veteran's Taxi Cab   552–1300
Yellow Cab   626–2345

Telegrams

See Telephone and telegrams.

Telephone and telegrams

See also Useful Telephone Numbers at a Glance.

Dialling codes

San Francisco: 415. (However, from September 1991 the 415 code will be split; the new 510 code will apply to the East Bay counties of Alameda and Contra Costa, encompassing Oakland, Berkeley, Concord, Pleasanton and Livermore).
To the United Kingdom: 011–44.
To Canada: as for a long-distance call within the United States (i.e. dial 0 followed by the local dialling code).

Tariffs

Local calls from coin-operated telephones cost 20 cents. Since these telephones do not accept coins larger than 25 cents, directly dialled long-distance (and in particular international) calls cannot easily be made from them. Nor can long-distance calls be made from post-offices. A reverse charge (collect) call can however be made from a coin-operated telephone through the operator. Hotels normally add a surcharge to the cost of a call so if you have a friend whose telephone you can use it is certainly advantageous to do so. Calls to all European countries cost per minute $1.42 from 6 p.m. to 7 a.m., $2.37 from 7 a.m. to 1 p.m., $1.78 from 1 to 6 p.m. plus tax. A three-minute call dialled direct costs $12.60 or $7.05.

Certain numbers (in the form 800–123–4567) can be dialled free of charge (e.g. for hotel bookings, information, etc.). Dial 1, followed by the number.

Toll-free calls

Telegrams generally have to be telephoned; there are very few telegraph offices where they can be handed in.

Telegrams

Television

See Radio, TV

Theatres

The American Conservatory Theater, San Francisco's Tony Award-winning repertory company, present a balanced mix of classical and modern drama, tragedy and comedy at the Stage Door, Orpheum and Palace of Fine Arts Theaters in a season that extends from October to May (tel. 749–2228 for programme).

The famous San Francisco Mime Company (tel. 285–1717) performs in the open-air during the summer and indoors (in theatres) during the winter.

The Curran Theater

Time

The following little theatres stage their own productions:
One Act Theater Company, 430 Mason Street, tel. 421–6162.
Eureka Theater, 2730 16th Street, tel. 558–9898.
Julian Theater, 16 Washburn Street, tel. 647–8098.
San Francisco Repertory Theater, 4147 19th Street, tel. 762–BASS.
Other theatres:
Curran Theater, 445 Geary Street, tel. 474–3800.
Geary Theater, 415 Geary Street, tel. 749–2228.
Golden Gate Theater, 25 Taylor Street, tel. 474–3800.
Magic Theater, Fort Mason, Building D, tel. 441–8822.
Mason Theater, 340 Mason Street, tel. 668–8862.
Marine's Memorial Theater, 609 Sutter Street, tel. 771–6900.
Orpheum Theater, 1192 Market Street, tel. 474–3800.
Presentation Theater, 2350 Turk Boulevard, tel. 752–7755.
Theater on the Square, 450 Post Street, tel. 433–9500.
Zephyr Theater, 25 Van Ness Avenue, tel. 861–6895.

To find out what's on, consult the dailies.

Opera, concerts ballet | See Music.

Time

San Francisco is on Pacific Time which is 3 hours behind Eastern Standard Time and 8 hours behind Greenwich Mean Time.

From the first Sunday in April to the last Sunday in October the time in force is Daylight Saving Time, an hour ahead of Pacific Time.

Tipping

In the United States a service charge is very seldom added to the bill so a tip has to be given.

Hotels

Bellboys are usually tipped $1 for each item of baggage.

At the end of a stay it is usual to leave the room maid a tip of 50 cents per day ($1 per day if the room is a double one).

If the doorman calls up a taxi for you he gets 50 cents or $1.

Restaurants

The usual tip is 15% of the bill, not including the 7.25% sales tax. The tip is always left on the table. In classy restaurants the maître (head waiter) also expects a tip.

Taxis

Taxi drivers expect 15% of the sum shown on the meter, and possibly a bit more for short trips.

Barbers and hairdressers

The usual tip is 15%.

Shoeshine

The usual tip is 25 cents.

Tourist Information

United States Travel and Tourism Administration, PO Box 1EN, London W1A 1EN, tel. (071) 439 7433.
No personal callers.

In the UK

San Francisco Convention and Visitors Bureau, 201 Third Street, Suite 900, San Francisco CA 94103, tel. (415) 974–6900. (Free maps, brochures, accommodation listings and events schedules.)

In San Francisco

The Bureau's Visitor Information Center is in Hallidie Plaza (lower level), at the intersection of Powell and Market Streets, tel. 391–2000.
Mon.–Fri. 9 a.m.–5.30 p.m., Sat. 9 a.m.–3 p.m., Sun. 10 a.m.– 2 p.m.
Closed for Thanksgiving, Christmas and New Year.
MUNI Metro: Powell Street.

Redwood Empire Association, 785 Market Street, San Francisco CA 94103, tel. (415) 543–8334. (Information on the entire Californian North Coast.)

Chronicle Cityline is a free 24-hour telephone information service (news, weather, sports, business, trivia and more); tel. 777–6035.

International Visitors Center, 312 Sutter Street, San Francisco, tel. 986–1388.
(Assistance to foreign visitors.)
Mon.–Fri. 9 a.m.–5 p.m.

Travel Phone USA is a free nationwide multilingual tourist assistance and information service to all visitors from abroad, tel. (800) 255–3050.

Dial 391–2001 (recorded message).

Day's events

Dial 673–MUNI or 788–BART.

Public transportation

Travel documents

Passports are required by all visitors to the United States except Canadian and British subjects resident in either Canada or Bermuda and returning there from a visit to a country in North, Central or South America. British visitors must have a regular 10-year passport: the one-year British visitor's passport is not valid for the USA.
Visas are not required by Canadian citizens; or British citizens providing they are staying in the USA for less than 90 days, and are in possession of an onward ticket issued by a carrier who has agreed to participate in the no-visa programme. Those unsure about visa requirements should call the US Embassy in London on (071) 499–3443 (recorded information) or (071) 499– 7010 to speak to someone.

Useful Telephone Numbers at a Glance

Airlines	
– British Airways	800–247–9297
– PanAm	800-221-1111
– TWA	800-221-2000
Embassies/Consulates	
– UK	981–3030
– Canada	495–6021
Emergency calls	
– Medical emergency, Fire department, Police	911
– Ambulance	931–3900
Information	
– Buses (long distance)	
Greyhound	433–1500
Trailways	982–6400
– Buses (local)	
A/C Transit	839–2882
Airporter (to the airport)	495–8404
Golden Gate Transit	332–6600
SamTrans	761–7000
– Events	
San Francisco Convention and Visitors Bureau	974–6900
The Bureau's Visitor Information Center	391–2000
Redwood Empire Association	543–8334
International Visitors Center	986–1388
Travel Phone USA	800–225–3050
Day's events	391–2001
In the UK	071–439–7433
BART (Bay Area Rapid Transit)	788–BART
MUNI (Municipal Railway Company)	673–MUNI
Weather forecast	936–1212
Time	767–8900
Lost Property	
BART	465–4100
Rail services	
AMTRAK Transbay Terminal	800-872-7245
Southern Pacific Railroad	495–4546
CalTrain	800–558–8661
Telephone	
– Information San Francisco	411
– Information California	555–1212
– Information USA	Area Code + 555–1212
– Information abroad	0 (operator)
– Dialling code UK	011–44
Telegram	648–4100

Weather reports

The periodic newscasts on radio and TV (see entry) include updated weather reports and forecasts. Call 936–1212 for Bay Area weather.

Weights and measures

1 inch=2·54 cm	1 mm=0·039 in.	Length
1 foot=30·48 cm	1 cm=0·033 ft	
1 yard=91·44 cm	1 m=1·09 yd	
1 mile=1·61 km	1 km=0·62 mile	

1 sq. in.=6·45 sq. cm	1 sq. cm=0·155 sq. in.	Area
1 sq. ft=9·288 sq. dm	1 sq. dm=0·108 sq. ft	
1 sq. yd=0·836 sq. m	1 sq. m=1·196 sq. yd	
1 sq. mile=2·589 sq. km	1 sq. km=0·386 sq. mile	
1 acre=0·405 hectare	1 hectare=2·471 acres	

1 cu. in.=16·386 cu. cm	1 cu. cm=0·061 cu. in.	Volume
1 cu. ft=28·32 cu. dm	1 cu. dm=0·035 cu. ft	
1 cu. yd=0·765 cu. m	1 cu. m=1·308 cu. yd	

The US gallon and other measures of capacity are smaller than the corresponding British (Imperial) measures, one US gallon equaling 0·83 British gallon. The following metric equivalences are for the US units.   Liquid measure

1 gill=0·118 litre	1 litre=8·474 gills	
1 pint=0·473 litre	1 litre=2·114 pints	
1 quart=0·946 litre	1 litre=1·057 quarts	
1 gallon=3·787 litres	1 litre=0·264 gallon	

1 oz=28·35 g	100 g=3·527 oz	Weight
1 lb=453·59 g	1 kg=2·205 lb	
1 cwt=45·359 kg	100 kg=2·205 cwt	
1 ton=0·907 tonne	1 tonne=1·103 tons	

The US hundredweight is smaller than the British hundredweight (100 lb instead of 112 lb), and the US ton is the short ton of 2000 lb (compared with the British long ton of 2240 lb and the metric tonne of 1000 kg – 2204 lb). The metric equivalences given above are for the US units.

Temperature

Fahrenheit	Celsius	Conversions
0°	−18°	$°C = \dfrac{5(°F - 32)}{9}$
10°	−12°	
20°	−5°	$°F = 1.8 \times °C + 32$
32°	0°	
50°	10°	
68°	20°	Ratios
86°	30°	°C: °F = 5:9
95°	35°	°F:°C = 9:5

Youth Hostels

YMCA	YMCA Central Branch (105 r.), 220 Golden Gate Avenue, tel. 885–0460. YMCA Embarcadero Branch (275 r.), 166 The Embarcadero, tel. 392–2121.
YWCA	YWCA Hotel, (40 r.), 620 Sutter Street, tel. 775–6500.
Youth hostels	San Francisco International Youth Hostel (165 beds), Building 240, Fort Mason (Bay Street/Van Ness Avenue), tel. 771–7277. Golden Gate Youth Hostel (60 beds), Sausalito, Building 941, Fort Barry, tel. 331–2777.

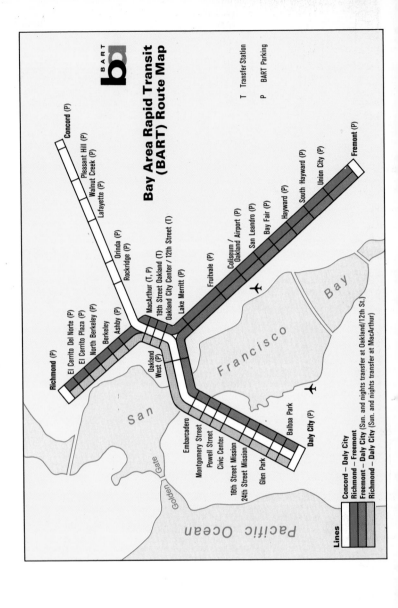

Bay Area Rapid Transit (BART) Route Map

BART

T   Transfer Station

P   BART Parking

Concord (P)
Pleasant Hill (P)
Walnut Creek (P)
Lafayette (P)
Orinda (P)
Rockridge (P)

Richmond (P)
El Cerrito Del Norte (P)
El Cerrito Plaza (P)
North Berkeley (P)
Berkeley
Ashby (P)

MacArthur (T, P)
19th Street Oakland (T)
Oakland City Center / 12th Street (T)
Lake Merritt (P)

Oakland West (P)

Fruitvale (P)
Coliseum / Oakland Airport (P)
San Leandro (P)
Bay Fair (P)
Hayward (P)
South Hayward (P)
Union City (P)
Fremont (P)

Embarcadero
Montgomery Street
Powell Street
Civic Center
16th Street Mission
24th Street Mission
Glen Park
Balboa Park

Daly City (P)

San Francisco Bay

Pacific Ocean

Golden Gate

Lines

Concord – Daly City

Richmond – Fremont

Fremont – Daly City (Sun. and nights transfer at Oakland/12th St.)

Richmond – Daly City (Sun. and nights transfer at MacArthur)